THE
WAY
OF THE
PHOENIX

S TEPHEN H. P ROVOST

ISBN: ISBN: 978-1-7320632-2-8

For the seekers..

With thanks to my talented wife, Samaire, for editing this work, offering some excellent suggestions, catching the odd typo (well, a few typos that were occasionally very odd indeed) and, most of all, for her love and support.

Prelude

The language of sacred texts, at its best, is both poetic and compelling. It invites the reader to think both deeply and without guile, exploring life's grandest complexities and its most charming simplicity.

The use of proverb and parable to express wisdom has long interested me. Though followers in some traditions take their scriptures literally, the most profound - in my opinion - know how to express and interpret their insights allegorically. While the literal may touch on a single point in history, the allegorical can transcend the bounds of a given context and speak to audiences across the ages. This is why Aesop's fables, the fairytales of the Brothers Grimm, the parables of Jesus and many of the ancient myths that survive in numerous cultures are timeless. They never happened, but they're always happening, alive in archetypes that survive centuries and millennia. They're stories of heroism, relationships, honor, justice and fortitude that are told to children in their youth and retold to those children's children as the years pass.

No one takes the parables of Jesus, for instance, to be literal or historical, any more than we would the stories of Aesop. We're told up front that these are parables, and we read them as such. Yet tales of talking snakes and donkeys - characters that would have seemed right at home in Aesop's imaginary worlds - are taken as anything but imaginary by many today.

Let me, therefore, be clear on the nature of this present work: Nothing presented here actually happened. The parables - or Tales, as I call them - do not involve historical figures. The proverbs (or Teachings) weren't inscribed in stone by a divine hand, delivered by an angel or dictated by a shaman in a state of ecstasy. The words are entirely my own, though the ideas behind them are far older than I am. This is not because they are divinely inspired, but rather because they have been part and parcel of shared human experience for thousands of years and more. The themes of justice, fellowship, communication and peace are universal and are addressed here, just as they have been addressed by the Buddha, Lao Tzu, Hillel, Marcus Aurelius, Socrates, Shakespeare and many others throughout history.

The Tales (parables) in this work are modeled on fables and allegories offered by everyone from Jesus to Aesop to Hans Christian Anderson. There's a message, or moral, to each one of them. The Teachings (proverbs) are similar in style to those often attributed to King Solomon, Lao Tzu, Confucius, Jesus and others who sought to communicate wisdom in succinct, yet thoughtful sayings - nuggets of transcendence in the simplest of forms.

The Tales and Teachings you are about to read are not a matter of commandment - but of one writer's creativity and conscience. I sought to include and illustrate ideas based on the principles of respect, compassion and common sense. So if you find yourself nodding along and saying to yourself, "I knew that," it's probably a good sign.

That said, I certainly don't expect everyone to agree with everything written here, any more than everyone can (or should) agree with every point or precept set forth in any volume of this nature.

The present volume is a companion piece to a previous work on the life of Jesus, titled "The Gospel of the Phoenix." The style is purposely similar, as is the presentation. It is not, however, in any sense a sequel and does not deal with Jesus the Nazarene at all. The previous work incorporated various existing traditions regarding Jesus into a framework based on my own research and interpretation. By contrast, none of the content in this book can be attributed to anyone other than the author. These sayings and stories were never shared by Jesus, Aesop or anyone else. They're appearing here for the first time.

You'll catch glimpses on the pages ahead of thoughts that might seem at home in fairy tales, Zen proverbs, Gnostic texts, Christian writings and secular philosophy. My inspirations are diverse, as are the subjects covered here.

Happy reading.

The Book of

Tales

(or Parables)

1
Origins

[1] In the beginning was Peace.

[2] And Peace was divided, giving rise to Fulfillment and Want.

[3] Want, in her lack, gave rise to a single one, Hurt.
[4] Fulfillment, in her abundance, gave rise to Repose, Indulgence, Greed and Hubris.

[5] Then Hurt gave birth to Bitterness, Anger, Sorrow and Confusion.

[6] These and the children of Fulfillment made war upon one another. [7] Confusion in jealousy assailed Repose, and Hubris met Anger on the field of battle. [8] Bitterness lashed out against Indulgence, and Greed sought to visit despair upon Sorrow.

[9] In these times, Repose was vanquished. In these times, Hubris and Anger mocked each other, locked in a battle neither could win, with each becoming more like his adversary as the fight raged ever onward. [10] Bitterness grew more bitter, and Indulgence allied herself with Greed.

[11] But Greed and Sorrow both increased.

[12] In time, the cacophony of their quarrels drove out Peace from their presence, and she withdrew to a place apart from her children, cradling to her bosom the slain child named Repose.

[13] The others barely noticed Peace's departure, for they had long ignored her counsel. [14] In time, outside her presence, they forgot both her ways and her example, knowing not whence they had come.

[15] But Peace took a new name, Memory. And she dwelt not among them.

2

The Five Creatures

[1] Four creatures found themselves together at the beginning: the eagle, the dolphin, the lion and the dragon.

[2] Each was asked which portion of the earth would be his, and they divided the realms among them. They drew lots, and the dragon chose first. [3] Said he, "I shall choose the realm of fire, for with it I shall destroy my enemies!"

[4] And it was granted.

[5] Then came the lion's turn, and he said, "I shall choose the realm of earth, for the earth shall tremble

at the sound of my roar, and none will dare to stand against me!"

⁶ The next lot fell to the eagle, who proclaimed, "I shall choose the air. For no one knows where its next breath will take it, and in mastering it shall I become master of all I survey!"

⁷ When finally it was the dolphin's turn to choose, she was overjoyed to find that the realm she had sought as her own was the one that remained - the realm of the waters. ⁸ And she said, "No one can fathom her depths, no one can stand against her tides and no one can grasp her essence with their fingers." (For which reason she did not take fingers to her form, but fins).

⁹ When all these things had been decided, a fifth creature arrived among them standing on two legs. ¹⁰ This one was told that, because he had come late, no realm remained to assign him. But he became wroth at this and would not accept it.

¹¹ So he went to the lion and said, "See how much greater the dragon is than you are because of his fire!" And the lion roared loudly, declaring, "None is greater than I!" ¹² When therefore the dragon came to sleep upon the earth, the lion buried him under a mountain. And there the dragon remains to this day, belching fire in his rage at the sky.

[13] Then the two-legged creature went to the eagle and said, "Behold! The lion has subdued the dragon, who has defiled your realm with smoke and fire!"

[14] The eagle answered him, saying, "Am I not greater than the lion?" And he built a nest around the lion's head as a collar, and no matter how mightily the great beast shook his head, it held fast in its place.

[15] Then the two-legged creature went to the dolphin and declared, "See how the eagle lords it over everyone from his perch on high? How can we teach him a lesson?"

[16] But the dolphin said, "You are worthy to teach no one, Two Legs. For your ways are the ways of war, and I want no part of your lessons. [17] Behold! My realm covers all of the sea. What is the land in comparison?" And with that, he swam away.

[18] Then the two-legged one became master of the land, for he used the lion's collar to subdue him while the dragon slept under the earth. [19] The eagle thought to challenge him, but realized the other had tricked him into waging war against his friend, the lion, and contented himself with the realm of the air.

[20] The dolphin took counsel with them and said to them, "The two-legged one will make war on his own kind, now that he has no one else to left to provoke. [21] But we must be wary, lest he again seek to ensnare us in the net of his ambition, or lest his own wars lay waste to all the earth."

[22] The others were in agreement. And from that day forward, whenever the two-legged one approached, they fled and hid themselves. [23] It is not because they are afraid, but because they did not trust him to recognize their beauty or understand their wisdom.

3

The Man and His Problems

[1] A certain man dug a hole in which to bury his problems, piling them up at the edge. But he dug it so deep that he found he could not climb out again.

[2] What happened then?

[3] All the problems that lay at the edge of the chasm fell in upon him, until he was buried beneath them.

[4] No one ever heard from him again.

4

The King and the Temple

¹ A great king said to himself one day, "Behold how greatly my god has blessed me! Therefore shall I build a wondrous temple in his honor."

² He conscripted slaves to cut down the trees of the forest and mine the quarries in the hillside. Then he levied a tax upon the people, so he could employ the greatest craftsmen from lands near and far.

³ These built for him great columns in the likeness of the trees he had cut down, but when the birds of the forest built nests in them, he chased them away. ⁴ They fashioned tables and an altar from the stone mined in the quarry. But when the men who had labored sought to rest on them, he had them shackled.

⁵ At last, the craftsmen decorated the entire temple with the likeness of pomegranates and vines, and of the moon and the stars in the heavens. But the people hungered because of the taxes he levied, and a loaf of bread became as rubies to them, a sheaf of wheat like spun gold.

⁶ When all was completed, the king stood back and marveled, saying, "Truly have I fashioned a wondrous tribute to my god!" Then did he betake

himself to his bedchamber and rested from his labors.

⁷ In the night, there came a dream to him, and his god stood tall before him in the image of a woman. ⁸ "What have you done?" she demanded. "You cut down my forests to build a forest of your own, then deny the birds of the air their solace. ⁹ You overturn the earth, my resting place, yet deny rest to those who labor. ¹⁰ You set up images of fruit and bounty, yet deny these very things to those who hunger.

¹¹ "Behold this abomination. You have created a sanctuary for your own conceit and a house for your own adoration. Such a place I will never inhabit. ¹² You have defiled my true temple and made a false one to fleeting glory."

5

The Rich Man and the Island

[1] A certain rich man lived in a faraway city. Whenever he walked on the streets, the poor would come up to him and beg alms, and he would toss them a coin from his pocket. [2] At length, however, he grew weary and said to himself, "If I did not appear so rich, these people would stop bothering me." So he began dressing in plain garb, but the poor still recognized him and approached him seeking alms.

[3] After a time, he decided, "These people will leave me alone if I am no longer wealthy." So he loaded his entire fortune onto a boat and took it to an island, where he hid it safely away so no one could find it.

[4] When he returned, however, the people still sought alms from him. [5] When he said, "I am no longer rich," they told him, "You are lying! We know you have been rich from birth. Do not deceive us!"

[6] They would not believe him but instead petitioned him all the more. [7] When at last he could endure no more of it, he betook himself to the harbor, thinking that he might go forth again to the island and retrieve his fortune to placate them. [8] Yet when he arrived at the shore, his boat had been laid

waste by the waves of a great storm and naught was left but planks floating on the water.

[9] Having left his money on the island and having no way to reach it, the wealthy man was now destitute. [10] He therefore returned to the streets of the city and began to beg alms there. [11] But the poor still recognized him and spat upon him, saying, "Do you dare take alms that are meant for us that you may line your coffers further? Begone from here and leave us to our misery! Do not inflict your own beside it!"

[12] They drove him off from there, and none of the rich would give him any solace, for they knew him also as a selfish man and a spendthrift. And they too, believed he was seeking to line his pockets further at their expense.

[13] In time, the man's days came to an end. And he was cast out to sea in a small boat that came to rest on the very island where his fortune was buried.

[14] The one who has ears to hear, let him hear.

6

The Watchman

[1] There lived a certain nobleman who was afraid of the king and wanted to protect his household. [2] He therefore went forth into the village and inquired among the townsfolk whether there were any who would be willing to guard his land.

[3] Several men came forward, and he chose one from among them to serve as a watchman. [4] "If anyone should come here unbidden," he told the man, "be certain that he does not leave alive."

[5] The man agreed and stationed himself inside the doorway to the man's home, where he waited day and night.

[6] One evening, while the nobleman was asleep, a stranger came through the door unbidden. [7] The watchman set upon him and beat him with his fists as he cried out in protest, then killed him with a blow to the head.

[8] The nobleman, hearing the commotion from his chamber, hurried to find out the source of it. [9] When he saw what had happened, he fell to the floor and prostrated himself, for there in the doorway lay the body of his only son.

[10] "What have you done?" cried the nobleman.

[11] The watchman said, "Just as you had bidden."

[12] The man, who was a widower, died without an heir, and the king seized all his assets. [13] Then the king said to the watchman, "Come and stand guard for me. For I can be sure that you will do as you are bidden in all things."

[14] And he gave him three times the salary the nobleman had paid him.

[15] When, the next day, the watchman came to take up residence in the palace, the king gave him a hearty welcome. [16] Then, knowing that the watchman would follow his instructions to the letter, he told the man, "Let no man enter my drawing room unbidden, save my only son, should he ask it."

[17] The watchman nodded. When the chamberlain came to the king's drawing room, he was turned away. [18] When the privy counselor came to the king's drawing room, he was rebuffed. [19] But when the king's son came to the king's drawing room, the watchman admitted him, just as he had been instructed.

[20] The prince entered that chamber and slew his father, and the next day he was crowned the new king. [21] But he dismissed the watchman, saying to himself, "Any fool could have seen that I did covet my father's throne. Were this man truly loyal, he would have betrayed my treachery."

²² The watchman, having failed to prevent the king's murder, lived out his years in disgrace. But the treacherous prince, because of his cunning, prospered all his years upon the throne.

²³ So discernment serves the faithful and the faithless in equal measure, and trust misplaced is the undoing of them both.

7

The Price of Happiness

[1] There lived a man in a certain city who spent a lifetime accumulating wealth, thinking it would make him happy, yet all the gold in his treasury failed to brighten his countenance.

[2] He therefore sought out the oracle of that city and asked her, "Tell me, wise oracle, what may I do to be happy?"

[3] She told him, "Hoard not your fortune, but spend it freely."

[4] And he thanked her.

⁵ Then the man went forth and spent freely on wine and carousing. He bought for himself fine garments of silk and satin, and he purchased for himself a large estate with vineyards and stables. His home he furnished with fine couches, marble tables and expensive draperies.

⁶ At the end of this, though, he still despaired. So he returned to the oracle and said to her, "I did as you instructed, yet still I am miserable. Tell me, can my wealth truly be exchanged for happiness?"

⁷ She told him, "There is a certain man who stands near the back of the market every day selling vegetables. Go to that man and say to him, 'I wish to purchase happiness.' He will show you."

⁸ And he thanked her.

⁹ Then the man went forth as she had instructed and found the man with the vegetable cart at the back of the market, just as she had said. ¹⁰ He said to the merchant, "Good sir, I wish to purchase happiness."

¹¹ The merchant smiled at him and said, "This day, you are in luck! Come with me!"

¹² And the man followed the merchant away from the market and down a country lane to a small hovel next to a graveyard. The stench from the graveyard was such that the man held his nose as he passed by it, and he wondered what it was that lay ahead.

¹³ The merchant bade him step inside the hovel, and there he was greeted by a single spare room with

wooden planks covered with straw that served as beds for the merchant, his wife and their two daughters. [14] A single table stood near a stove in one corner, and a draft blew in from the window.

[15] At the merchant's arrival, his wife stepped forward to greet him, smiling as she fastened her arms about his shoulders. [16] His daughters stood where they were and came running over to tug at his sleeve.

[17] That evening, the merchant and his wife prepared bread and lentil soup, and their visitor declared it the best he'd ever tasted. [18] The merchant regaled his family with the story of his day, and they responded in kind. "Our friend," he said, "was sent to me, just as the oracle predicted," the merchant said.

[19] The visitor was puzzled. "Did you also visit the oracle? And what was your question?"

[20] The merchant laughed and answered: "I asked her why money brought such sorrow," he said.

[21] "Did you get your answer?" the visitor inquired.

[22] "Indeed," said the merchant. "If not for your wealth, you would not be here with me this evening. For you would have kin of your own to tend to, a wife to love and children to raise. Instead, what have you but your money?"

[23] The visitor nodded and said no more.

[24] When, at last, it was time for him to depart, he said, "How may I pay you for your kindness? The oracle said I might exchange my wealth for happiness, and happiness in your company did I find."

[25] But the merchant shook his head and said, "Your payment is made already. The wealth you exchanged was the pleasure of your fine company this evening. As to your money, I want it not. I have treasure of my own that far exceeds it."

[26] Thus was the oracle's word fulfilled.

8

The Seeker of Wisdom

[1] A certain woman went forth in search of wisdom. She went first to the priest and asked him, "How shall you answer my question?" [2] And the priest pulled out a book and began to quote from it. [3] The seeker listened for a time, then asked the priest, "Who is it that wrote that book?"

[4] "A great man who lived long ago," said the priest.

[5] The seeker said, "Did you know his man?"

[6] The priest laughed and said, "Of course not, for he lived many years before I was born."

[7] So the seeker told him, "I came seeking a living word from your lips, but you have given me instead the words of a corpse." And she went her way.

[8] Next the seeker went forth to the halls of government and asked the prefect of that province, "How shall you answer my question?"

[9] And the prefect said, "Wait for a few moments, while I consult with my counselors as to the proper response."

[10] The seeker said, "Do your counselors speak for you?"

[11] The prefect said, "Of course not, for they are appointed to do my bidding."

[12] So the seeker said to him, "I came seeking wisdom from the mind of a leader, but I see I have come to the wrong place." And she went her way.

[13] The seeker went next to the prefect's counselors and said to them, "How shall you answer my question?"

[14] But they said, "Ask the prefect, for he is the one who rules over us."

[15] She then told them that she had come from the prefect himself, but they said, "We only tell him that which he wishes to hear."

[16] So the seeker said to them, "I came seeking advice, for I was told you were advisors, but I see I have come to the wrong place." And she went her way.

[17] Next the seeker went to an oracle, reasoning with herself, "Surely the prophet will know the path of wisdom." And she asked the prophet, "How shall you answer my question?"

[18] But the prophet's response was vague, so she said, "How are your words to be interpreted?"

[19] The oracle said, "Howsoever you wish," for the prophet had no answer, yet also had no wish to appear ignorant.

[20] So the seeker said to the prophet, "I came seeking the path of eternity from the heart of a seer, yet I understand now that the seer is blind." And she went her way.

[21] Next the seeker went to the arena where all the people of the city were gathered. And she called out, "Good people, how shall you answer my question?"

[22] But they heard her not, for her voice was drowned out by the cacophony of their own shouts and whistles as each cheered on their favorite in the games.

[23] The seeker said to herself, "I came seeking wisdom from the people, yet they are divided against themselves. How can they find wisdom if they will not listen?" And she went her way, going finally to her home.

[24] There she sat alone and asked, "Shall my question ever be answered?"

[25] And in silence, the answer came.

9

The Traveler

[1] A traveler went on a journey, eager to reach his destination. Through many storms he persevered, keeping his eyes always on the road ahead and his mind ever focused on the goal before him: a gleaming golden city with crystal fountains and rainbow skies. [2] He had been told so much about it, he was eager to see it for himself.

[3] But when at last he came to the end, he found nothing as he had imagined it. Instead, a boulder lay at the end of the road, beside which stood a tiny shack that was boarded up and empty. [4] No one was there to greet him, save only a single watchman.

[5] The traveler said, "I expected something else."

[6] And the watchman replied, "You missed it."

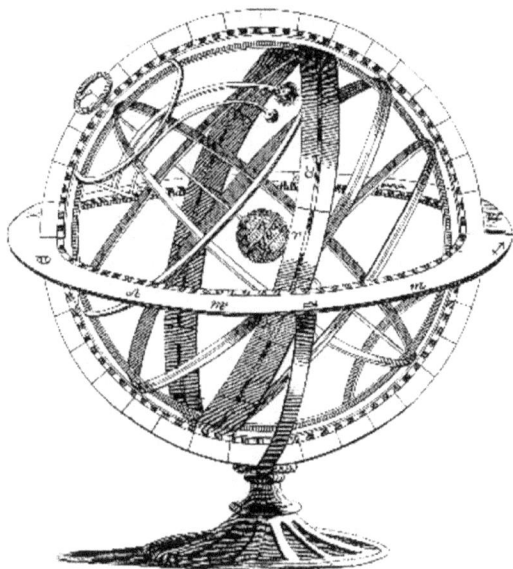

10

The Ends of the Earth

[1] The people of a village asked the priest of that place, "Have you seen the ends of the earth?"

[2] The priest threw his cape back with a flourish and said, "But of course!"

[3] So the people said, "Show us."

[4] But the priest said, "It is far away. Only a priest is fit for such a journey. You would surely not survive it."

[5] Then a young man among them stepped forward who was strong of heart and full of vigor. His arm

was stout and his legs had run many miles. [6] He said to the priest "I shall accompany you."

[7] The priest began to protest, but it became clear that the young man would not be dissuaded and the others among them were extolling him for his courage.

[8] The priest therefore took the young man out of the village to shouts of acclaim and great hope.

[9] The two of them went forth past the gates, past the farms and meadows and out into the wild that surrounded the village. [10] They traveled for many miles, and after the first day, the young man asked how close they were to the ends of the earth. But the priest said, "We will get there when we get there." So they went forward.

[11] After the second day, the young man asked the priest the same question, and the priest gave him again the same answer, for he hoped that the young man would grow weary of the journey and reach the end of his patience. Still, the next day, they went forward.

[12] As sunset approached on the third day of their journey, it was the priest who had grown weary. His legs had become weak and his chest heaved with exhaustion, for he was neither strong of heart nor full of vigor, as the youth was.

[13] So after a time, he stopped in a clearing between two groves of trees, picked up a stick from the

ground and traced a line in front of them from one end of the clearing to the other. [14] He declared, with a great deal of pomp and circumstance, "Here it is. We have come to it at last. Behold! The ends of the earth!"

[15] The young man, though, looked beyond the line the priest had drawn and saw there a stand of oak trees and blooming flowers, rocks, an anthill, a fallen log and a small deer grazing. [16] He therefore said to the priest, "I perceive the earth continues beyond this place."

[17] But the priest said, "You are surely mistaken."

[18] Then the young man asked himself, "Shall I believe the priest or shall I believe my own eyes?" And having decided at last in favor of the latter, he went forth and took a step across the line the priest had drawn.

[19] Then he opened his mouth and spoke to the priest, saying, "What place is this that I now stand, if it is beyond the ends of the earth?"

[20] The priest's eyes grew wide, for he was amazed. The priest's mouth fell open, for he was astonished. [21] Then he said to the young man, "You have become a ghost and you have made yourself a demon. Because you have stepped beyond the ends of the earth, you may nevermore return to the realm of the living. Henceforth are you banished from this world."

[22] He uttered an invocation to shun him, then he turned his back to him, shook the dust off of his feet and went his way.

[23] The young man remained there for a time, uncertain about what he should do. But after some consideration, he grew tired of standing in solitude and stepped back across the line the priest had drawn.

[24] Sensing nothing had changed because of his brazen act, he set out to travel back the way he had come and arrived after nearly three days at his village. [25] He was on his way back to his own home when the priest spied him and gasped in horror, shouting for all to hear, "It is the ghost of the young man who fell off the ends of the earth!"

[26] The youth opened his mouth to protest, but before he could remove himself, the priest's acolytes and others of the townsfolk surrounded him and laid their hands upon him, holding him fast.

[27] "Take this demon again to the ends of the earth and remove him once and for all from the land of the living," the priest demanded, "for he is but a ghost who will haunt us if we suffer him to remain in our midst!"

[28] They did as he bade them, forgetting that the priest had formerly told them such a journey was beyond their capacity to endure. [29] Ushering the young man once more out of the village, they set out

to return him by force to the place where the priest had first taken him. [30] The youth objected loudly, saying, "If I be a ghost, how is it you can handle my flesh? And if I be a demon, wherefore can you bind me?"

[31] But such was their fervor and devotion to the priest that the heard him not - or if indeed they heard him, they paid him no heed.

[32] The priest led the rabble back to the place where he had drawn the line, which now was faded from the wind and from animals passing to and fro across it.

[33] When they arrived, they bound the young man with strong rope and sinew. Then, at a word from the priest, they cast him over the line (making sure not to cross it themselves) and began to build a high wall along the length of it.

[34] They labored for days, then weeks and then months to complete it, until it encircled the village and the surrounding countryside completely.

[35] From that time forward, no man ventured beyond it, and no one from outside came in.

[36] Many years passed, and the priest died, as did his acolytes. [37] The hunters from the village slew every beast of the forest, for there were not enough within the wall to sustain the village and produce sufficient young that their kind might endure.

[38] The village grew poor or lack of trade and thirsty when its wells used up their water.

[39] At length, everyone in the village perished, and the wall in time began to crumble. [40] Then did others come to seek their fortunes, and they remembered the tales of the village as it had been. These tales had been told to them by the descendants of their first king - a man sent in exile from that village in a time of legend.

[41] They remembered his tale and, when they came to the place where the village had once been, they founded it anew and named it in his honor.

[42] Thenceforth did it prosper.

[43] But no one remembered the name of the priest.

11

Two Fathers

[1] A teacher told his acolyte this parable:

[2] Two men lived in the same village. The first was a prosperous nobleman, the second a drunkard and a wastrel.

[3] The first man had several children and gave them all they wanted. If his daughter wished for fine clothing, she would have it. If his son asked for a well-bred stallion, it was his. [4] Yet when he grew old and feeble, and asked his children for a simple favor, they forsook him. They squandered all he had given them, and when he went to his rest, they laid him in a pauper's grave.

[5] The second man, likewise, had children. But he abused and berated them so they cowered in his presence. Whatever they sought from him, he withheld, and instead spent what he had on carousing and drunkenness.

[6] Despite all this, his children grew up to be successful craftsmen and traders. Yet whenever their father demanded that they serve him, they would do so without question in the vain pursuit of his favor.

[7] When at last he died, his children buried him with dignity and great honor.

[8] So it is that a kindness withheld is often more powerful than a kindness freely given.

[9] When the parable was finished, the acolyte asked his teacher, "Is there no justice in the world?"

[10] But his teacher said to him, "It is the lot of men and women to bring forth justice. It is our lot to establish and preserve it. Where we confer it not, it is absent; where we preserve it not, it perishes."

12

The Nature of the World

¹ A king wanted to know the nature of the world, so he called four wise men before him and asked his question to each of them in turn.

² The first bowed before him and said, "Good king, the nature of the world is manifest for all to see. It is first of grain, then of wood, then of stone, then also of iron."

³ The king thanked him but did not approve his answer.

⁴ The second wise man then came before him and bowed at his throne, saying, "Good king, the nature of the world is manifest for all to see. It is composed of living spirit in four forms, the fire that is passion, the air that is breath, the water that is sustenance and the blood that is life.

⁵ The king thanked the second wise man also, but neither did he approve this answer.

⁶ Then came the third wise men into the king's presence. Bowing before him, he said, "Good king, the nature of the world is not fully manifest. It is composed of members too small to discern when separated, yet when brought together they become visible, more vast than the sands on the seashore."

[7] The king thanked the third man, as he had the first two, but though he saw merit in his words, neither did he approve this answer.

[8] Then the fourth wise men came before him, and the king asked him the same question. [9] "What you ask is a difficult question," he said, "for each man and each woman creates a new world. [10] The one who loves builds a world from joy and from kindness, from respect and understanding. The one who hates builds a world of sorrow and cruelty, of disdain and ignorance."

[11] The king thanked him and said, "You have answered well. Now assist me in building a world out of love."

13

Two Gods

[1] An acolyte went to his teacher and asked her, "What is the nature of a god?"

[2] She answered and said to him, "One man said the sun was his god, so he sat all day in the field gazing up into its radiance. A second man believed his god was invisible, so he sat all day at an altar worshiping him. Can you tell me the difference between them?"

[3] The acolyte said, "The first is a fool, for he shall surely be blind by the end of the day. The second is a wise man, for he is pious and holy."

[4] "But the second man shall also be blind," said the teacher. "For he sees nothing save the altar before him. [5] He sees not the changes in the tides nor the leaves changing color on the trees. He sees neither his neighbor's strife, that he may console him, nor his joy, that he may join in celebration. He sees only a cold stone altar."

[6] The acolyte asked, "How then is one such as myself to learn of his god's ways?"

[7] And the teacher said, "It is not given for us to see the face of a god, any more than it is given for us to look into the face of the sun. The sun illuminates all that surrounds it; so it is also with the divine. They reveal all that they survey. [8] If, therefore, you wish to see a god, look all around you at what is made manifest by the light of wisdom. And if you wish to be like a god, reveal wisdom to others."

[9] The acolyte then went his way. He nevermore visited the altar, and the world was the better for the wisdom he shared.

14

The Six Prophets

¹ The queen of the land called together all those who claimed to be prophets and said to them., "How will your god prove himself to me?"

² The first prophet declared, "He will send down fire from the sky!"

³ The second proclaimed, "He shall bring forth rain upon the land for forty days and forty nights!"

[4] The third said, "He shall cause the womb of a barren one to be with child."

[5] Another said, "He shall cause the queen to prosper in all she does."

[6] And still another said, "He shall go forth before you into battle, and you shall claim a mighty victory."

[7] Finally, the last of the prophets stood before her, and she asked him also, "How will your god prove himself to me."

[8] But the prophet said, "Wherefore should a god prove himself to a mere mortal? In promising such, each of these others has proven his own god false. [9] Consider this: If their promises fail, they prove nothing. Yet if they are fulfilled, it is from chance or deceit, for no true god need prove himself. [10] My god resides not in bluster, but in silence."

[11] She marveled at his answer and dismissed the other prophets from her sight.

[12] But the last prophet departed of his own accord, for liberty is the child of wisdom.

15

The Lesson of the Traveler

[1] A teacher told her acolyte the following parable:

[2] A traveler came upon a man bowing before a shrine alongside a great river.

[3] "Why do you bow before this shrine?" the traveler asked him.

[4] The man replied, "Because it is holy."

[5] The traveler said to him, "Come with me. I will show you things you will never see if you remain beside the river."

[6] But the man thanked him, but declined his offer, and the traveler went on his way.

[7] Sometime later, after he had crossed high mountains and seen magnificent waterfalls, after he had broken bread with peasants and princes, the traveler returned the way he had come. [8] When he happened upon the place beside the river, he found the man he had met earlier, bowing before the same shrine.

[9] The traveler was surprised to find him still there, so he asked the man, "Why is this shrine holy?"

[10] The man answered and said to him, "Beause the scripture so declares it."

[11] Then the traveler looked at the man and asked him, "Why do you believe the scripture?"

[12] The man looked at him, puzzled, and said, "Because my master has declared it."

[13] The traveler then approached and said, "May I see this scripture of which you speak?" whereupon the man produced a scroll: taking it gently from beneath his cloak, he handed it to the traveler.

[14] But instead of opening it to read the words within, the traveler took the scroll and flung it into the river.

[15] Its owner looked at the traveler with dismay and asked him, "Why have you done this thing?"

[16] And the traveler said to him, "So that you might come with me on my journey. There are many scrolls that speak the same as this one, and I shall obtain for you another when we reach our destination."

[17] But the man's eyes only widened, and he said to the traveler, "What you have done is a sacrilege. You shall pay for your crime with blood." And he drew his sword.

[18] In that moment, the traveler vanished from before his eyes. [19] The man called out for his master, but no one answered. He waded into the river in search of the scroll, but he could not find it. He bowed before the shrine, seeking revelation, but none came to him.

[20] When the teacher had finished her parable, she spoke to her acolyte and asked him, "Which of these two men has given the greater offense?"

[21] The acolyte responded, saying, "Surely, it is the traveler. For he has interrupted his neighbor's devotion, desecrated the scripture and spurned the teachings of a master."

[22] But the teacher said, "Was not the greater offense given by the man at the shrine? For did he not offend his own spirit by declining the traveler's offer? [23] Had he accepted his invitation, he would have crossed high mountains and seen magnificent waterfalls; he would have broken bread with peasants and princes; he would have been enlightened, and his wisdom would have been magnified. Yet he chose instead to remain in ignorance."

[24] The acolyte was astonished and asked his teacher, "But what of the scripture and the shrine and the master? Should their lessons be so quickly discarded?"

[25] The teacher smiled and said in reply, "The greatest lessons are those lived, not those filtered through mind of another. [26] A shrine is never holy; it is but a symbol of that which is. A scroll is never sacred; it is but a symbol of sanctity. So it is also with the master and his words.

[27] "Those who worship the vessel ignore the truth contained within it. They are as those who stand in the gateway, so captivated by its magnificance that they cannot pass beyond it. [28] The vessel becomes their tomb, the shrine a monument to their folly."

16

The Queen's Heir

[1] There lived a queen who was without an heir, so she sent forth a herald to all the people of the land and said to them, "Whichever one of you can describe me most accurately shall be become the heir

to all my realm. Come, therefore, and answer for me this simple question: Who am I?"

[2] Many people came from far and wide and assembled before her throne one by one, each hoping to answer her correctly.

[3] The first was a baker, and she said to the queen, "A good and noble queen such as you, I surely know your tastes!"

[4] But the queen answered, saying, "Have you not seen the people of the village - the farmers and the craftsmen and the merchants? They eat milk and porridge each day. How is it that I should have sweets while they partake of gruel? [5] Nay, no queen should prosper so while her subjects are wanting. I am neither good nor noble, but my taste is to become such." So the queen dismissed the baker.

[6] The next was a soldier, and he said to the queen, "A brave and mighty queen are you! Your army is fierce, made in your image. And your courage is beyond dispute."

[7] But she answered, saying, "Have you not seen the enemy slain in battle? We have taken them from their families by the force of our hand. Our own have fallen also, leaving widows and orphans to beg for their keep. [8] Nay, what you have seen is not courage, but cowardice. True courage stands fast against the violence men inflict upon one another. True courage defends the widow and orphan, it does not tear them

from their households. [9] I am neither brave nor mighty, but I seek to become such." So she dismissed the soldier.

[10] The next was a carpenter, and he said to the queen, "A woman such as yourself must appreciate fine art, for you surround yourself with the finest woodcarvings in all the land!"

[11] But she answered him, saying, "The forests of my realm once were home to fox and ferret, to squirrel and starling. Yet now they have fled because of the woodsman's axe. [12] These woodcarvings of which you speak were once a living home to the hart and hedgehog. Yet now they are dead and taken from their rightful place. The art you see before you is but a perversion of its true beauty. [13] Had I appreciated the artistry of the forest, I would not have let this happen." So she dismissed the carpenter.

[14] Finally, there came before her a peasant girl who was nearly grown.

[15] The queen asked her, as she had asked all the others, "Who am I?"

[16] But the peasant girl said to her, "Forgive me, but I do not know. I came from the village, where my father was a blacksmith. He went away to fight the enemy, and he never returned. [17] My mother sent me to the forest to gather pears and gooseberries and walnuts. But where the trees had been were only

stumps, and the woodsman's axe had laid the forest bare. My journey led me here, for we are hungry."

[18] The queen said to her, "You shall have the choice of all the food within my realm," and bade her come forward to the throne.

[19] Then the queen stepped down from the dais and yielded her chair to her. "You have much to learn," she told the girl, "but the lessons your life has taught you are those I am in need of." [20] So saying, she went away from that place and never returned. And from that day forward, the peasant girl ruled the land fairly and wisely. [21] She called the army home from battle and planted new trees in the forest. And every morning for breakfast, she served milk and porridge with her own hand to all the members of her court.

17

The Woman and the Merchant

¹ A young man went forth to the village square, where he saw a woman whose face was not veiled, whose head was uncovered and whose ankles were bare. He thought to himself, "She is seeking to attract a man," so he approached her.

² When he greeted her, the woman told him he was mistaken and sought to return to her business, but the man persisted.

³ She therefore told him that she wore no veil because she wished to see clearly, she wore no head covering because of the warmth and she wore no ankle covering because she did not wish to stumble over the hem of a long garment.

⁴ Yet he did not believe her.

⁵ So he laid his hands upon her and sought to take her with him by force, but she raised her voice so that a crowd gathered around about them. ⁶ Still, no one in the crowd moved to help her, and the man who had lain hold of her cried in a louder voice still, "She has provoked me!" and "This is my right!"

⁷ But just then a merchant stepped forward, the richest man in all the marketplace. He said to the man, "I would speak to you."

[8] The young man felt proud at being recognized by so distinguished a person and thinking that the wealthy merchant meant to reward him in some way. So he stopped his yelling, but still held fast to the woman.

[9] The merchant said to him, "Tell me, are you the one who stole twenty pieces of gold from my stall when I left it unattended?"

[10] The young man's face turned pale, and he said, "Of course not! Why would you think such a thing of me?"

[11] "In all my time at this market, I have never heard a man speak the words that you have spoken," the merchant said. "You said, 'She has provoked me.' [12] Is it not natural that I should assume you believe my gold coins provoked you, as well? If you wish to take this woman who does not belong to you, would you not also take my money were you given the chance, saying I had provoked you to do so?"

[13] The young man was speechless.

[14] The merchant then said to those assembled, "This man has nothing to say in defense of himself." [15] Those who were in authority came and took him into custody, whereupon he was charged with both assault upon the woman and thievery of the merchant's gold.

[16] The woman thanked the merchant for his courage, but he said to her, "It is not I who showed

courage, but you yourself. For I have gold and am known throughout the village, yet you who are without money and known to but a few stood up for what is virtuous."

[17] And from that time forward, all the women of that village wore their heads uncovered and disdained the veil; neither did they care to cover their ankles. [18] And no man dared question their honor, because none could match either their confidence or their courage.

[19] Time passed, and hours became days, which in their turn became years. The woman who had been confronted in the marketplace had a daughter, and her daughter had a daughter after her.

[20] The young woman, however, was modest and humble, and when she visited the marketplace, she adorned herself as the women of old, so that the people turned their heads to see her. [21] A veil was drawn across her face, and a cloth obscured her brow. A long and flowing robe fell down across the entire length of her body, so that it nearly swept the ground as she passed by.

[22] The townsfolk had forgotten that all women once had dressed this way, and they mocked her, saying, "She is hiding some disfigurement," and "She must be hideous!"

[23] The grandson of the man who had once assailed her grandmother still lived in that place, and when he

spied her passing by, stepped forward to confront her. [24] In rudeness and presumption, he put his hand forward to remove her veil. But she drew back from him, saying, "It is not your right to do this!"

[25] Soon, others gathered around them and took the young man's part. They remonstrated with the woman, saying, "What is it you are hiding? Do you have a demon?"

[26] But she said to them, "My body is my own, to reveal when I choose it. You are the ones who obey a demon, for seeking to annul my choice and make it be your own. [27] You are nothing but thieves and hypocrites. Would you have me draw back your coats and pull down your trousers? Go your way, and leave me to my peace."

[28] They marveled and could say nothing to this, and one by one, they went their way.

[29] The veil is but a piece of cloth, and the skin is likewise but a covering. Regard them not of much importance, but rather the heart of the person which lies beneath them.

[30] The one who has ears to hear, let him hear.

18

The Faithful Dog

[1] Six shepherds took their flocks to pasture in the rolling hills many miles from the city. There they found a great expanse of grassland, and their sheep had more than their fill.

[2] The shepherds were content until it came about that a pack of wolves came down from the forest and attacked the flocks. Five of the shepherds lost many sheep, but in the morning they noticed that not a single sheep from the sixth man's flocks was missing.

[3] They therefore went to the man and said, "What sorcery is this? How is it that the wolves have taken

so many of our sheep, yet have not harmed a single one of yours?"

[4] But the sixth shepherd said, "Friends, it is no sorcery. The wolves visited my flocks in the night as well, but my sheep were well guarded by my shepherd dog, Arturo."

[5] Then the other men became jealous and said, "We do not believe you. We believe your good fortune is the work of a demon. If indeed your dog is such a fine protector, let him protect our flocks, as well!"

[6] So the shepherd said, "As you wish."

[7] The next night, however, the wolves returned. And though Arturo chased most of them away, he could not be in so many places at once. [8] When he fought off one of the wolves from the north, another came in from the east. And when he guarded the eastern edge of the grassland, another attacked from the south.

[9] One of the wolves came upon him from the west, and would not yield, sinking his teeth into the flank of a large, plump lamb. So Arturo growled and leapt upon him, fighting him fiercely until the wolf at last drew back.

[10] But when the owner of the sheep heard the sound of the wolf howling, he rushed out to find the sheep lame and Arturo's coat strewn with blood.

[11] He therefore cried aloud, saying, "See what this dog has done? Now we see who the real demon is!"

[12] He went to the others and told them this, and together they made their way to the house of the sixth shepherd in order to accuse him.

[13] "What treachery is this?" they demanded. "Your dog is the one who was attacking our flocks all along. This is why none of your sheep were killed!" [14] They then beat the shepherd with their fists and stoned Arturo until he was so badly hurt he could no longer raise his head. Then they went back to their own fields, congratulating themselves for having preserved their flocks from such a demon.

[15] But that night, the wolves came again, and neither Arturo nor his shepherd was there to oppose them. [16] The wolves came in and devoured as many sheep as they could eat, for indeed it was a great feast. And when morning came, the shepherds were all dismayed.

[17] They said, "What is this evil that has befallen us? Surely that devil of a shepherd and his hound from hell are behind this. They have struck out now at us in retribution, as is the way of evil men. We should never have shown them kindness or mercy!"

[18] They picked up sticks and stones, and they went straightaway to the shepherd's home, where they slew both the man and Arturo. Then they returned to their

own fields, saying to themselves, "Now, we will know peace at last, and our flocks will prosper."

[19] Yet again, the wolves returned, taking even more of their sheep, so that they became despondent and said, "Behold, the demons haunt us even from the grave!" But they knew not what more they could do. [20] From that time forward, the wolves feasted every night, until not a single sheep remained in the fertile fields.

[21] So it was that the five shepherds lived the rest of their lives as beggars and as paupers, never understanding that they had slain the ones who tried hardest to help them. [22] For such is the way of men: they see what they want to see and believe what they wish to believe, regardless of what the truth might be.

19

The Pilgrim

[1] A woman lived on the side of a hill in the high mountains when the rains came. The sky fell down in streams and torrents, until it loosened the earth on the hillside, and it came crashing down on the woman's home.

[2] Her parents and children, who lived there with her, were spared. But her husband fell dead as the earth consumed him, and their home was utterly ruined. [3] She and her family had nowhere to lay her heads and no roof to shelter them from the storms to come.

[4] Knowing not what she should do, the woman went to the village priest and asked, "How could the gods have allowed such a thing?"

[5] But the priest answered and said to her, "Who are you to question the gods? Repent of your pride, lest you be cast down into the pit. [6] It is your own lack of faith that has brought this thing upon you. Had you not dared to question the gods, surely they would have watched over you."

[7] The woman began to cry, and she went from there, disconsolate, feeling the weight of sorrow heavy on her breast.

[8] After a time, she met a hermit by the side of the road, deep in meditation. The woman asked the hermit the same question. "How could the gods have allowed such a thing?" and said to him also, "What should I do?"

[9] The man inclined his head toward her in greeting and said, "Who knows the mind of the gods? They do as they will, and I fear a humble man such as I cannot answer your question. [10] Betake yourself instead to the wise teacher. You must travel many miles from here on a great pilgrimage to reach her, but perhaps she will have the answers you seek."

[11] Then he told her of the place that she should seek, and showed her the beginning of the path that led there. "You will find the wise teacher tending to her garden, and she will welcome you with kindness."

[12] The woman thanked the man and went on her way, gathering up what few belongings she still had

and taking her mother, her father and her children along with her.

¹³ So did she become a pilgrim.

¹⁴ They traveled many miles, away from the tall mountains that had been their home, across wide rivers and fertile valleys, through pastureland and forest and barren desert. Then at last they reached the place the hermit had described. ¹⁵ She found the wise teacher, just as the hermit had said, tending to a small garden behind a cottage with a thatched roof. Her skin was dark and wrinkled, and her hands were withered yet strong.

¹⁶ When she raised her head to meet the pilgrim and her family, her lips did not smile, but her eyes were radiant.

¹⁷ "You have come far," she said. "Your garments are worn, and your bodies are stooped. What is it you seek?"

¹⁸ "Wise teacher," said the pilgrim, "I seek an answer to my questions. We have journeyed to this place because we have no home, for the rains came, whereupon the hillside fell down upon my home and my beloved. And it consumed all that we knew. ¹⁹ Why have the gods done this thing to us? And what are we to do now? ²⁰ We built our home in the mountains for the safety they offered us against our enemies, yet now they have become our undoing. How is it that we may have the security we seek?"

²¹ The pilgrim looked at her and said, "Behold this young seedling."

²² She held up a fragile shoot of green, its tiny roots dangling from a small clump of dirt in the palm of her hand. ²³ "Tell me, where would this fragile sprout be without the rains? Would it not wither and perish in the heat of the sun? And would we not perish also?"

²⁴ The pilgrim nodded. "Then it is the sun that is to be blamed."

²⁵ But the teacher said, "Without the sun, the plant would also perish, as would we all. Deprived of the sun's warmth, how would we resist the snows of winter? And deprived of her light, how would we find our way amid the darkness?"

²⁶ The pilgrim had no answer.

²⁷ "You built your home in the mountains seeking security," said the teacher, "and now you come to me in search of how to obtain it. Tell me, then, what is the nature of this security you seek?"

²⁸ The pilgrim thought a moment and said, "I wish for everything to remain the same."

²⁹ The teacher smiled and inclined her head. "If the eye never opened, it would not see. If the child never grew, she would not learn. If the night never ended, we would not know the day. If the shoot never blossomed, it would not produce fruit. ³⁰ Tell me, then, do you really wish for all things to remain

the same? For if no thing ever changed, the neither would you perceive it, and then you would be dead."

[31] The pilgrim knew not what to say. She closed her eyes, then opened them, gazing on the tiny shoot in the teacher's hand.

[32] Then the teacher said to her, "Come, let us speak no more of such things. Now is the time to take our sup. Sit at my table, and partake of my garden's bounty. Then I shall make a place for you and your family to rest this night."

[33] The pilgrim nodded, grateful for the teacher's hospitality, for she was indeed weary and in need of nourishment. [34] They all ate a hearty meal and slept well in the teacher's cottage, so that when they awoke the next morning, they were rested and refreshed.

[35] The pilgrim sought out the teacher to thank her for her kindness, but she was nowhere to be found. Instead, there was only a note upon the table. [36] It read: "I have waited long for one such as you to seek me out - one open to hearing the truth, though it be painful, and one in need of renewal. [37] Now renewal has come to us both. This day, I depart for a new life, I know not where. To you, I gift this cottage and garden. and I am grateful for the gift of your friendship."

[38] So did the teacher become the pilgrim, and the pilgrim, having learned from her, became the teacher.

20

The Debaters

[1] Two men stood in the town square debating. The first was saying, "Faith leads to wisdom! Believe first, then you shall see!" But the other was saying, "Wisdom leads to faith! He who seeks understanding builds the foundation for belief."

[2] Many people gathered around to hear them, until the square was overflowing with the thoughtful and the curious.

[3] The first man said to them, "Tell me, is it not true that those who seek wisdom are always left wanting more, while those of faith are at once fulfilled?"

[4] The other answered him, saying, "Those who see what they wish to see are indeed fulfilled, yet blind themselves to all else. And worse: what they wish to see may be but an illusion."

[5] Then he said also to the first man, "Tell me, if faith precedes wisdom, how is it that one decides where to place that faith? [6] Does he accept the faith of his fathers or his homeland? Is he convinced by miracles and answered prayers? If so, does one god answer prayers more often than another? If it is so, I wish to hear of it."

[6] "Surely," answered the first man, "such wisdom comes by way of revelation."

[7] "Then you admit that wisdom comes first."

[8] The man shook his head. "It is a different sort of wisdom. It is divine wisdom. The ways of heaven are not the ways of men."

[9] "Do you intend to say," asked the second man, "that true wisdom is guised as folly?"

[10] "Indeed," said the first. "It is often thus."

[11] "So whatever seems wise to me I should discard, that I may receive the proper faith?"

[12] "Yes."

[13] "But I have faith that the sun will appear on the morrow, because it has been so each day throughout my life. I have faith that rain will fall in the winter, for thus has it always been. I have faith that the moon will wax and wane in its due course, because I have observed it. [14] Would you have me believe that the sun would hide her face from us in the morning? That the rain will cease falling? That the moon will go forever dark? Simply for the sake of faith?"

[15] "If it is so revealed, then of course."

[16] "And who is to reveal it? A priest? A king? A scribe? If such ones ask that we believe a thing that is foolish, I must at once ask whether they do so to further their own cause. For either they have renounced the ways of wisdom because they are

foolish, or they have adopted the ways of folly to some purpose."

[17] "The purpose," said the first man, "is to further the cause of faith."

[18] The second man looked to the skies and frowned, then fixed his gaze once more upon his opponent. "I will ask you once again: How does one decide whether to place one's faith? [19] The priests of one god declare a certain thing, and the priests of another say something different. Without wisdom, how is one to decide whether the one or the other seems more reasonable? Or should I merely choose that which appears more foolish?"

[20] "You must choose that which is truly revealed."

[21] "By whom? By the priests? The scribes? The king? Even now, is not wisdom still required?"

[22] But the first man's eyes narrowed and said to the other, "Wisdom is but a trap set by the beguiler. Trust not your own understanding, but yield to the one who is greater. I perceive you have a demon."

[23] The second man laughed. "Have not you yourself said that folly appears as wisdom, and wisdom as folly? Therefore, what you perceive as a demon could indeed be the image of your own god. [24] Regardless, why should I - or any of these good people - credit the words of a man who admits he speaks but folly?"

[25] With those words he left the place. And the crowd was amazed at what he had said.

21

The Mountain

[1] A student asked her teacher, "What is the world like?"

[2] And the teacher said, "The world is like a hill, and the world is like a valley. On the hill live all the kings and nobles, the wealthy men and generals. In the valley dwell the poor and the hungry, the laborers and ploughmen. On the top of the hill lie many stones, which are greatly valued."

[3] "Stones?" asked the student.

[4] "Yes, stones. The men on the hilltop roll them down with a single push, and those in the valley, through great toil and effort, seek to return them to the top again."

[5] "But why?" asked the student.

[6] "Because," said the teacher, "those at the top of the hill demand it."

[7] The student was puzzled at this, for, she wondered, why would the people of the valley not simply refuse?

[8] At this question, the teacher bowed her head and replied, "They dare not, for fear that those on the hilltop will cast more stones down upon them, and they will be buried underneath a multitude of rocks and rubble." [9] She paused and laid a hand on the student's shoulder. "And because they live in hope that, should they reach the top themselves, those already there will reward them with a place of their own."

[10] The student looked into her eyes and asked, "If the stones are of such great value, why do those on the mountain not simply hoard them for their own pleasure? Why do they bother to push them over the edge?"

[11] "Because they fear the people of the valley would rise up and make war upon them, and that without the stones to encumber them, they would ascend in force against them." [12] She smiled and asked her student, "What wisdom do you glean from this tale?"

[13] Her student thought for a moment and said, "It is always easier to push a rock downhill than it is to raise one up!"

[14] The teacher laughed. "Indeed, it is. And the world is oft unjust in this regard."

[15] The student shook her head sadly. "Then what are the people of the valley to do?"

[16] The teacher's expression grew earnest and her tone sober. "They must learn that their true masters are not the men on the top of the mountain, but rather their own fear and the false hope to which they cling. [17] Then can they proclaim their freedom - as can you, dear child."

[18] "But how?" asked the student.

[19] "Take the stones cast down upon you and build a mountain of your own, then share it with all who care to ascend it."

[20] The teacher handed the student a single stone, and the student went her way.

22

The Suitors

[1] Three men sought a woman's hand in marriage. The first was a rich merchant who said to her, "I will shower upon you all the gifts your family could never give you. If you marry me, you will never want for a single thing. [2] I shall show you the wonders of all the world and you shall never have a care for what you shall eat or whether you shall have a roof over your head. [3] Your fare shall be the rarest of delicacies, and your roof shall be carved from the finest cedar."

⁴ He bowed before her and kissed her hand, saying, "Give me your answer in a fortnight, that I may plan for our future together."

⁵ The second man who came before her said, "My lady, you are the most radiant vision I have ever beheld. Your virtues are more numerous than the stars, and your beauty outshines the sun. ⁶ My need of you is such that I would be destitute without you. Should you consent to be my bride, I will be ever loyal and never forsake you."

⁷ He prostrated himself before her and kissed her feet, saying, "Pray, give me your answer on the morrow, for I cannot bear another day that we are parted."

⁸ The third man who sought her hand then said to her, "Behold, I am content in life. Should you spurn me, I will not grieve, but should you accept me, more content still shall I be. ⁹ I cannot offer you a vast estate or fine linens, nor will I affirm you in all things. Nay, I shall challenge you should you offend me, and shall expect the same of you."

¹⁰ Then he said to her, "By your leave," and at her nod, embraced her.

¹¹ She said to him, "When do you require an answer?"

¹² And he answered, "Whenever you have one that is true and well-considered."

¹³ The woman then sought out her mother, desirous of her counsel.

¹⁴ "Which man should I marry?" she asked her. "What of the first man?"

¹⁵ But her mother asked her, "Are you a trinket or bauble? This is how the first one will treat you. He has enough of these already, so how greatly will he value you? ¹⁶ Only a man without a heart offers ornaments to one he wishes to make an ornament herself!"

¹⁷ "Very well, then," said the woman, "what of the second suitor?"

¹⁸ But her mother asked her, "Is he a slave that he wishes to bind himself to you in servitude? Bound indeed shall you be, but *you* shall come to do *him* service, for he cannot manage it himself. ¹⁹ Only a man without a mind of his own offers unquestioning devotion. Truly, such devotion will be a millstone around your neck!"

²⁰ The woman frowned at her mother and then said, "What of the third man?"

²¹ Her mother smiled at this and said, "The one who embraces you is the one most to be considered. Yet consider also this: You are not bound to marry. ²² Make the choice which seems best to you, my daughter, even if that choice be none at all."

²³ The woman did not marry the first man. Many years later, she happened upon him and found him

destitute, whereas she had acquired a bounty without benefit of his affections. [24] He had parted with his whole fortune in an effort to purchase the one thing his wealth could not procure for him. After that, she never saw him again.

[25] The woman did not marry the second man. One day, she saw him following a woman down a certain path. He was always asking some favor of her, and a frown seemed ever knit upon her brow. [26] She never regretted spurning his flattery, for her own esteem was far preferred. After that day, she saw him no more.

[27] As to the third man, she saw him every day and they became the best of friends. Did they marry? That is another tale.

23

Two Sorrows

[1]A man asked his teacher, "Which is the greater sorrow - the one who has much wealth yet does not share it or the one who would share, yet has no resource?"

[2]"Truly," said the teacher, "the first sorrow is far greater. [3]The hoarder of gold will share nothing of value. Yet the one who is generous, though he has neither gold nor silver, will share from the bounty of his heart. And such, indeed, is the far greater treasure."

24
The Foolish Fathers

[1] A great general fathered a son, but his beloved wife died in childbirth. [2] As the boy grew, the man was often engaged in great battles and had no time for his son. The boy vexed him sorely, for he lacked discipline, as is the way with children. [3] So the man took to beating the child, telling himself, "The boy is unafraid of his own folly; in this manner shall I impart to him understanding."

[4] But when the boy came of age, he had learned to fear only his father's hand, and the beatings, which seemed wrathful and capricious.

[5] When the time came, the young man left his father's care, vowing never to return and taking with him the whole of his inheritance. He shunned the way of the soldier, for he loathed it, yet he was ever restless and found no solace in the world. [6] His father's harsh corrections had not redressed his folly, but had instead preserved it, for now he feared nothing save scorn and disapproval.

[7] The young man sought in vain to please all men and grew bitter when they, too, abused him. Soon, in his quest to gain their favor, he had surrendered every coin of the wealth his father had given him.

⁸ Yet as fortune would have it, in the course of time, the young man found a woman and loved her, and she returned his ardor. She was a woman of some means, and they lived without want in consequence.

⁹ In the course of time, she came to be with child, but like the young man's mother, she died giving birth to a son. The man was therefore left to care for the boy by his own hand alone.

¹⁰ He swore to himself that never would he strike the child, as his own father had done, but would instead protect him from all that was cruel and evil in the world. So the boy was brought up lacking nothing, and his father guarded him from every care. ¹¹ But the boy, like his father, grew up mindless of his own folly. He feared not the hand of his father, yet neither did he fear the world's harshness.

¹² When the time came, he too struck out on his own. And it came to pass that he, like his father, grew bitter when men abused him and when the world grew cold and distant.

¹³ So did the man who was brought up in fear and the man who was shielded both come to the same end. ¹⁴ False security is a door with a broken lock, unbarred against future hardship. ¹⁵ Fear rightly held is a true guardian, but fear misplaced is the gatekeeper of sorrow.

¹⁶ He who has ears to hear, let him hear.

25

The King's War

[1] A king bent on conquest sent great armies against his neighbors, who in their turn mustered armies of their own.

[2] The people said to him, "We are afflicted by this war, for we are bereft of those who provide for our sustenance. Not enough of us remain to pull in the harvest. Their food is not on our tables, but their

blood is spilled on your battlefield. We beseech you, good king, recall them, lest we starve."

[3] But the king said, "The lands to the east are green and fertile. Once they are ours, your bounty will increase. Fear not, for your harvest will increase tenfold once we have prevailed."

[4] The people then said, "What good will that be to us if we are dead? [5] Yet if you are determined to pursue this quest, at least send your own son, whom you love, to lead our children into battle. Then shall we know, as a token of good faith, that you will honor your word to us."

[6] But the king grew wroth with them and cursed at their demands, saying to himself, "Would they be king in my stead? What right do these commonfolk have to make such demands of me?" [7] Then he issued a proclamation, saying that no one should speak of this thing again and keeping his son from the battle thenceforth for as long as he should live.

[8] The war then raged for many years, and the children of the land were slaughtered so that there were not enough hands to till the soil, and it turned fallow as the nation's sons and daughters perished. [9] But as to the king's own son, not a hair on his head was harmed.

[10] And it came to pass that the young prince thought to himself, "Behold, no man in the world can

hurt me. Do I not deserve to sit on my father's throne?"

[11] He therefore went forth and took counsel in secret with men he could trust, and arranged to have the king put to death, that he might supplant him.

[12] So it was that the king who sacrificed so many sons and daughters of the people, yet sought to spare his son, was slain by the hand he had preserved.

[13] But it was not long before the people rose up against the new king and removed him from power, for the one who sacrifices others in the cause of vanity oft seals his own destruction.

26

The Problem of Evil

[1] A lame student came to his teacher one day and asked him why he had been born with a withered hand.

[2] "Some say it is because my parents did evil," he said. "Others because I have done evil. Others still because the gods are displeased with me."

[3] His teacher shook his head. "It is not because of any of those things."

[4] A shadow fell across the student's countenance, for he did not understand. [5] And the student grew displeased with the teacher, saying, "Then it is a grave injustice, and I am due recompense. Do you not see it, good teacher? Should this outrage not be avenged? What of justice? What of karma?"

[6] Then the teacher set before him a wooden box and brought forth a handful of round balls. Handing one to his student, he said, "Cast this now into the box."

[7] The student did as he had been bidden, and he watched as the ball bounced slightly sideways, then back up to him so he caught it.

[8] "This is what would happen if you were the only person in the entire world," his teacher said, and

handed him another. "Now, he said, drop both in the same instance."

[9] The student did so. One bounced true, and he caught it up in his good hand, but the other bounced askew off the side of the box, so that he could not retrieve it.

[10] "This is what would happen if you and I were the only two people on the earth."

[11] The student frowned, but the teacher smiled at him. "Now imagine there are a thousand thousand thousand balls. Can you foresee how many different places each one might land?"

[12] The student shook his head. "I cannot."

[13] "How, then, can you hope to predict the ways of karma? And how can you think to explain why a thing happens the way it does?"

[14] But the student had no answer. "There are too many possibilities," he said, and his face became downcast. "It is beyond the abilities of a simple man such as I."

[15] The teacher laughed. "You are no simple man, my friend," he said. "Nor am I. Yet for all my years receiving instruction, and more years still of observing life, such questions are far beyond my ability to answer. [16] It is natural for a man to think that, when he takes a single action, it will produce a certain outcome, as though a line were drawn from one point to another. [17] Yet each action is a current

that flows outward from the center, encountering other currents, waves and ripples as it advances. It touches not a single point, but every shore it reaches, and those on every shore are changed in consequence. [18] If you can predict such things with surety, you are a wiser man than I, and, indeed, wiser than the wisest ones in all the earth."

[19] The student went his way and was content. And from that point forward, his withered hand was not a cause of questioning, but a means of understanding.

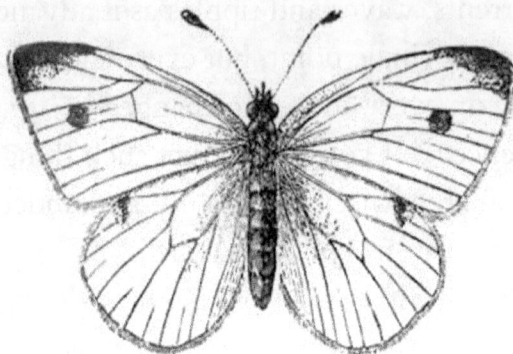

27

The Seventh Sigil

[1] Long ago, in a time of antiquity, there arose a great empire that was long at peace. Each day was much the same as the last, and all its citizens did their part that the land might prosper.

[2] Some were craftsmen, some were merchants, some were soldiers, some priests, some laborers and some rulers. These were the six vocations, and each had its own sigil.

[3] The symbol of the priesthood was the falcon, which flew between heaven and earth. [4] The symbol of the craftsmen was the beaver, for its industriousness. [5] The seal of the rulers was the elephant, for it was the largest of all earthbound creatures. [6] The sign of the soldiers was the dragon,

for its ferocity. [7] And the sigil of the merchants was the fox.

[8] The laborers had their own sigil, as well. Their symbol was the earthworm, for its lowly station.

[9] In time, the people grew so accustomed to their way of life that they enshrined these six into the book of their law. [10] It was decreed that a certain portion of their number would be assigned to each of the five great vocations, and those who failed would be consigned to the office of the poor.

[11] Much debate took place on how the members of each rank were to be chosen. [12] Some suggested birthright, that the sigils be passed down from the first generation onward. Others said the priests and rulers should choose, and still others that the members of each class should choose apprentices.

[13] They could come to no agreement. So it was suggested that a certain number of lots bearing the sigil of each station be placed into a drawing, and that every person in the realm be called upon to draw from a great barrel when they were of a certain age. [14] And each would then receive the animal that was the symbol of their station.

[15] Of the rulers' lots, there were the fewest, and of the laborers', there were the most. [16] Each person aspired to draw the elephant sigil, though many also sought the fox and the falcon. But none desired the earthworm.

[17] It came to pass that a certain young woman traveled from the far mountains to the capital for a drawing one year. She attended the drawing, as required, but said to those in charge, "Pardon me, but none of these stations befits me."

[18] They only laughed at her, saying, "It is not for your good that this great ceremony is being staged, but for the good of the entire realm."

[19] To this she answered, "Is it not for the good of the entire realm that I pursue the station that most befits me? In this way, I would be the greatest blessing to all whom I encounter."

[20] But the men would not listen to her, saying instead, "You shall be trained for whatever role you may choose. Your hand shall choose it, and it shall become a part of you, as surely as are the hairs on your head." [21] Then they took her to the barrel and demanded that she choose.

[22] She became desperate, saying, "Can my fate be changed should I not do well in the role that is assigned me?"

[23] The men, however, answered her with a saying common among the people, "A fox cannot grow wings like a falcon, and an earthworm is ever an earthworm."

[24] Like many others that day, she drew the lot with the earthworm sigil, and was sent forth to a camp of miners whose task it was to dig coal from the root of

the mountains. [25] She was given these things to take with her on her journey: a knapsack with a change of clothes, a thick jacket, a pan for cooking and a single earthworm.

[26] This last creature was her only companion during the weeks ahead, and it grew quickly on the leaves she fed it. [27] She noticed its appearance was not entirely like those belonging to her fellow laborers, but she thought little of it until one day it disappeared into a silk cocoon.

[28] When this happened, she understood the truth of it - that she had been given not an earthworm, but a caterpillar. [29] The other laborers saw this thing and marveled, but she hid the cocoon away from the overseer, so he could not see it. Then she patiently waited until it broke forth anew as a butterfly with sparkling, many-colored wings.

[30] She brought it forth, but it did not fly away from her, and the one in charge of the miners caught sight of it and demanded, "Where did you get this thing?"

[31] Then she said to him, "It is the sigil of my station that was given to me when I was brought here."

[32] The overseer frowned, saying, "Never have I seen this before. Show me the earthworm you were given."

[33] But she told him, "Here it is." And the others confirmed it.

[34] "Behold," she said, "the sign of the artists. The butterfly. The seventh sigil."

[35] All those present saw it as a sign that a new station had been ratified by heaven. [36] Therefore was the woman taken to the high seat of the empire, where she was granted a place as the court's royal artist. Indeed, such had been the role she sought from the outset.

[37] She worked with diligence and great skill, so that every work she produced was a masterpiece.

[38] So greatly did she impress the high ruler that he swore to grant her a single blessing, whatever she might ask save the throne itself. And she asked of him, "Would that the drawing of lots be abolished, and that all the people of the realm may be trusted to pursue the station to which the most aspire."

[39] Her request was granted at once, and soon a new saying was heard across the land.

[40] "My worm may, in fact, be a butterfly. And if a fox seeks the wings of a falcon, then who are you to deny him?"

28

The Three Words

[1] A certain man had long been afflicted with a palsy, such that the side of his face drooped and distorted. [2] From childhood, the others in the village would deride and scorn him, and whenever he opened his mouth to speak, they heard nothing of what he said, though he spoke only three words.

[3] "Forgive us," they mocked, "for we cannot hear your words, so distracting is your face."

[4] He turned aside for them and soon stopped speaking altogether, so that those who made his acquaintance thought him mute. Yet secretly, he thought to himself, "If only I were handsome, then the people would listen."

[5] Then, one day, he awoke to find that the palsy had departed. Spying his reflection in a pool of water, he realized that not only was his affliction gone, but his countenance was entirely without blemish.

[6] Those who had known him before did not recognize him, and those who met him anew heaped praise upon him, saying, "Behold! What radiant features! Surely, this is the son of a god!"

[7] After a time, he even dared to speak again, but again, no one deigned to listen. Again, they told him,

as before, "Forgive us, for we cannot hear your words, so distracting is your face."

[8] And again he fell silent.

[9] In time, the years took their toll on his countenance, as they are wont to do with every man. His radiance faded, and he became simply a common-looking man, neither radiant nor afflicted.

[10] At last, he thought to himself, perhaps the people will listen to me. So he raised his voice once again, but once again, no one listened, for his common looks did not draw their attention.

[11] "Forgive us," they said, "for we did not hear your words, so common is your aspect."

[12] So he repeated the three words he had been speaking from the beginning.

[13] "Kindly show love."

[14] And still, no one heard.

29

The Moon, the Daffodils and the Candle

[1] A boy in the village heard from a storyteller that the moon was made of cheese. When, therefore, his father told him that cheese came from cows, he thought it a wonder.

[2] One night, when staring at sky, he noticed certain stars in heavens made the shape of a cow, and he imagined that the moon must have come from this place.

[3] He spoke excitedly of this to his father, but the man was hard at work and did not correct his son's exuberance. In consequence, the boy became

confirmed in his belief of it, through his childhood and beyond.

[4] When he grew to manhood, he recalled the cow and the moon and the heavens. He found a plot of land on which to grow grain and fruit trees, and he made a pact with the landholder to supply much of his crop in exchange for his tenancy.

[5] Once this was accomplished, and when the time was right, he purchased a cow. She gave him milk aplenty, of which he drank his fill and sold the rest. [6] But he knew naught of how cheese was made, so he reasoned that it must be given at the full of the moon.

[7] He watched long, over many months, but his cow gave only milk. [8] At last, distraught, he sold her, convinced she was afflicted with some malady that prevented her from bringing forth cheese.

[9] For a short while, he lived off the profit from her sale, but before long, it came to pass that this resource was nearly exhausted.

[10] About that time, it so happened that he met a man along the roadside, selling flowers. [11] "Behold the bright, gold petals of the daffodil!" he said. "If you purchase these, they will surely bring you fortune, their golden blossoms drawing to you golden coins, which shall enrich you."

[12] The young man was impressed at this and, taken in by the merchant's confidence, believed his tale. [13]

He therefore gave him the last of what he had earned from the cow that he might procure the flowers, along with an abundance of seeds.

¹⁴ He returned to his home straightaway, whereupon he uprooted the fruit trees and plowed under the grain fields that he might plant the flowers far and wide. ¹⁵ But in the course of time, their color faded, and the gold gave way to brown. The day came when they shed their petals, and the young man saw no golden coins.

¹⁶ Before long, he knew, the owner of the land would come calling and demand the grain he had plowed under to plant the flowers, and the fruit of the trees he had cut down.

¹⁷ Desperate, he sought out a book he had been given as a child and found a line from it, which counseled:

¹⁸ Find a candle, dark and red
Burn it long beside your bed
Your enemies, their blood shall run
Before the morrow's rising sun

¹⁹ The young man found such a candle and lit its taper, setting it at his bedside just as the book had instructed.

²⁰ But in the night, the hot wax dripped onto the pages of the book he had been reading. These pages soon caught fire, and the flames did spread as the

young man slept, until the entire house was ablaze with their fury.

[21] In a single hour, all was consumed.

[22] In the course of time, the landholder found another tenant - one who did not believe that the moon was made of cheese. Or that golden flowers brought forth coins of precious metal. Or that red candles could vanquish an enemy.

[23] He rose early by the light of the moon to tend his crops. [24] He planted golden flowers at the base of his fruit trees that the faithful honeybee might visit them. [25] Then, he collected the true gold the bees produced, the soft, sweet honey they brought forth, which he sold at the village market for a profit.

[26] Soon, he had saved enough to buy the land from its owner.

[27] As for candles, he used them only to read by, and he always snuffed them out before letting his eyelids close for the evening. [28] Their color mattered little to him, only the words their light revealed, which made him all the wiser.

30

The Blight and the Messengers

[1] A landholder set off on a journey of trade and commerce, leaving his sister to tend his fields.

[2] One afternoon, she found the beginnings of a blight upon his fruit trees. Not knowing the source of

it, she grew concerned, for the fruit was a goodly part of her brother's livelihood.

³ She inquired of those who tended the neighboring fields, but none could say the cause of it. She therefore reasoned with herself, saying, "My brother is a master gardener. Were he here, he would discern the cause of this blight and heal it. But since he is abroad, the whole crop may perish."

⁴ She determined to send a runner to him straightaway, bearing an urgent message to bid him return that the fruit might be salvaged. ⁵ But as it was nearing the harvest, no one among the landholders could spare any of their field hands to make the journey. ⁶ She therefore found a beggar by the town gate and said to him, "I will pay you handsomely if you tell my brother of these things."

⁷ To this he readily agreed, and set out on his way immediately.

⁸ When at last he found the woman's brother, the beggar sought to deliver the message as promised. ⁹ But when the landholder saw the man's rags and drawn countenance, he said to him, "You have come here to deceive me while I bargain for new fortune. Which one of my enemies has sent you?"

¹⁰ The beggar opened his mouth to answer, and said that the man's sister had sent him. But the landowner would suffer that he speak no further. ¹¹ Instead, he called upon the authorities and

proclaimed to them, "See this man here? He is a liar, sent by men to cheat me of my fortune. He speaks in my sister's name, yet I know him not. ^{12} Arrest him, therefore, and have him cast into your dungeons."

^{13} When the messenger did not return and the blight became worse on the leaves of the trees, the landholder's sister grew worried. ^{14} Fearing the first messenger had been waylaid, she sought a second for the task, but still no man of the village cold be spared to embark upon such a journey.

^{15} As chance would have it, a foreigner was in that place on a visit from some distant land far northward. ^{16} When the woman heard of this, she approached him, and he consented to bear her message, for he was young and keen to see the world.

^{17} She paid him well for his troubles and sent him on his way to the town where her brother had business, whereupon he began inquiring where the man could be found.

^{18} At length, he located the woman's brother and opened his mouth to deliver her message. But alas, the man would not hear him. ^{19} Instead, he said to the messenger, "Who are you, a pale-skinned northman, to intrude upon me thus?" (For the people of his own land were all swarthy in complexion.) ^{20} "Your kind are all layabouts and swindlers, every last one of you. You sleep the winter away because the sun never shines on your land! [21] Begone from my presence, or I shall sell you to the slavers."

[22] The northman, fearing for his safety, departed with haste, leaving his message undelivered, and went forth to continue his travels.

[23] By this time, all the fruit of the landholder's trees had turned rotten, and all the leaves had fallen away from their branches. [24] Soon, every last one of them had withered from the blight, and when he returned at last to discover it, he despaired greatly.

[25] "What has happened?" he asked his sister. "And why did you send no messenger? Had I known of this blight, I could have cured it. But as it is, my dealings abroad proved unfruitful, and now my entire grove is lost!"

[26] His sister told him that she had sent two messengers to him, but that neither had returned to her.

[27] It never occurred to the man that she was speaking of the beggar and the foreigner, for to his eyes, such were less than men.

[28] His fortune forfeit, the man was forced to sell his land for a pittance and seek a new means of supporting himself. It is said that, at the last, he became a messenger himself, but that no one listened to a word he had to say.

The Book of

Teachings

(or Proverbs)

1

Integrity

[1] The All is a singular, unified whole. It is not at odds with itself. The limits of each one's perspective create the illusion of conflict, when in fact, all things are in balance and harmony.

[2] Try as we may, we cannot oppose this. The human beast may cut down forests, topple kingdoms, plough up the earth and, through hubris, create a

wasteland. [3] But amid these things, the All just winks, knowing that we are a part of her.

[4] Who are we to oppose her? Within her womb, her heart and her mind lie worlds upon worlds uncounted, dying and being born across a tapestry beyond imagining.

[5] This world shall pass away, whether at our hand or through some other power. To the All, it makes no difference. Its end shall be but a moment in eternity, a gateway through which the All must pass in perpetual self-renewal.

[6] One may ask, "Can the All be destroyed from without?"

[7] Such a question has no meaning. For how can anything exist outside the All, which by her very nature is inclusive? [8] We are a part of her and cannot venture beyond her essence. We can only act in such a way as to help define her balance.

[9] This balance reflects her integrity. It is neither a cord pulled taut nor pool cold and stagnant, but remains in every way dynamic. [10] Its nature is change, and its symbol is the unified circle. Having neither beginning nor end, it is self-fulfilling and self-perpetuating. [11] Its names are the All, the Source and Completion. It is the beginning and the end, containing both but having neither, and even this symbol is wholly inadequate.

[12] Some call it "God," but such a name is inadequate. It is at once creator and creation, its emanations remaining a part of it.

[13] The All is harmony amid dissonance, constancy in chaos. Her face we see in glimpses and reflections, our perception ever incomplete and flawed. [14] For this reason, we remain humble and also vigilant: humble in the knowledge that we may never know the All, yet expectant that more will be revealed, even as her visage changes.

[15] The All is herself the very process of discovery – ever changing, always shifting as the desert sands that erase the traveler's footprints. Nothing remains as it once was. [16] Never achieved, she is always achieving.

[17] To our eyes, her essence seems chaos that may not be grasped. Yet our perspective is what deceives us. [18] From within, we see but fragments of the All, bits and pieces swirling in a maelstrom, frantic in their turbulence and unfinished in their aspect.

[19] Still, it is we who are unfinished, and the All is ever becoming, for life is transformation.

[20] Do not say to yourself that the All is never ending. Say instead, the All is ever beginning.

[21] Change is continual. The All is neither a line stretching forward nor a single point on that line, nor is it a circle or even a spiral, though these last are closer to its nature. [22] Still, the mind cannot contain it,

nor can any shape encompass it. It is always unfolding and ever transforming.

23 When this is understood, we free ourselves from the bonds of Now and take on the aspect of becoming.

24 We bow to past lessons but no longer serve them.

25 We welcome each instant, but do not lay hold of it.

26 We build bridges for the future without presumption.

27 No moment is separate unto itself, but the All flows in a single stream that transcends what we call time.

28 There are those who say that every road leads to a single summit, and there are indeed many such roads. 29 Yet some roads lead away from the mountain, and still others begird the base of it, but never ascend. If you wish to reach the summit, be sure the road you choose leads upward.

30 If all things are fated, nothing ever comes to pass, for it has happened already, and "already" has no meaning.

31 Love without kindness is not love.

32 Kindness without justice is not kindness

33 Justice without understanding is not justice.

34 Understanding without humility is not understanding.

[35] Humility without truth is not humility.
[36] Truth without love is not truth.

2

Perception

[1] Perception is that which grants us access to the All. If something exists apart from perception, can we know it? If it does not exist, even with perception, can we discover it?

[2] Without a doorway, no key will avail us. And without the key, the way is barred, as surely as if nothing lay beyond.

[3] That which is perceived is no more than the tiniest fraction of the All.

[4] Consider the dog, who cringes at the sound of a whistle no human can hear. To us, it is but silence.

[5] Consider the one who is blind and the one whose ears are deaf.

[6] Consider also the sound of the thunder, the voice issued forth by the lightning, which arrives long after his blade rends the night in two.

[7] Many things are seen, yet not perceived.

[8] Many things are heard, yet not noted.

[9] Many more still are felt, yet are ignored.

[10] Even those perceived are soon forgotten, save for a precious few. These are stored away and seldom brought to mind, unless the need arises or some new thing perceived recalls them.

[11] Memory itself may shift with time, fading with the passing years or taking forms far different with the turnings of each life's path.

[12] Memories shaped by fulfillment and regret are but ghosts and shades of times now past.

[13] It is not well to trust alone one's own remembrance; test it instead against the words of trusted companions.

[14] Perception shared carries weight and power, for good or ill. If true, it bolsters truth; if false, it creates an artificial truth of its own, a house of lies built upon deceit's foundation.

[15] Once the lessons of memory are corrupted, they are either lost or must be relearned. The cost is great, the sorrow needless.

[16] Those without scruple purchase the truth with fear and corrupt memory with spite, that they might enslave others to their will. The fear of evil robs them of their hope, and resentment steals their joy.

[17] Thenceforth shall they cling to such horrors as though they were precious treasure, pressing a bitter blade against their breast and wielding it with impunity against all those who dare defy them.

[18] Perception is the only gateway to the All, yet when twisted for gain or power, it leads only to oblivion.

[19] The one whose eye is ever upon a distant goal risks stumbling over unseen rocks along the path. The one whose eye is ever cast downward for fear of stumbling risks losing his way. Let not one eye be blinded by the other.

[20] The enemy close at hand distracts from a greater foe unseen … and from blessings nearer still.

[21] The seed planted in the heart spreads ever outward in shoots and branches, taking root and demanding nourishment. Kind multiplies after its kind.

[22] The joyful heart spreads joy.

[23] The angry heart spreads anger.

[24] The fearful heart spreads fear

[25] The compassionate heart spreads compassion.

[26] The bitter heart spreads bitterness.

[27] The mind creates divisions, some born of need and others of fear. The heart discerns the difference, and the All transcends their names.

[28] Power resides not in men, save when by men it is bestowed. Authority is given, honor is accorded and respect is proffered. [29] Some who earn these things rightly never receive them, for fools and despots withhold what is rightly theirs in service of their own lies.

[30] Fear is a sentinel, not a master. It keeps watch but should never command you.

[31] Pain is a fire to keep watch by. Yet left untended, it spreads and consumes the entire camp.

[32] Pain gives warning for those who heed not prudence. Yet sometimes, even the prudent must bear it, and even some who observe its counsel shall not escape its wrath.

[33] Decisions are steps, not conclusions.

3

The Earth

[1] There are those who say man was given charge
of the earth to rule over it, yet if this were true, would
the earth rise up against him? [2] The winds roar
mightily to drown out his commands. The sea rises
up and swallows his puny ships. The earth brings

forth fire from its depths to consume him, and the skies fall upon him in torrents.

³ Men raise their scepters upon the earth, and she laughs at their insolence. They build monuments to eternity, and she uproots them like weeds from her garden. ⁴ Your palaces fall to ruin, your inscriptions to glory worn away by wind and rain.

⁵ Even your gravestones are cracked and weathered. Soon they will return to the earth itself, leaving no record your sojourn.

⁶ But grieve not, for all things pass away, yet even so are renewed.

⁷ Creation did not come to pass in six moments, in six days or in six thousand thousand years. It occurs in every moment, renewing itself in color and pattern, in sound and in silence, from the moment that was to the moment that will be and onward.

⁸ Indeed, it is far easier to tear down than to build up, so the building must always continue. In the same way, it is far easier to wage war than to preserve peace, so trust need always be fortified.

⁹ There are those who say that men have been given dominion over the beasts of the field. Yet men are but beasts in their own right. Wherefore should they have dominion?

¹⁰ Have you given birth to the cattle? Does your blood run through the hawk or serpent? If you have not given them life, who are you, then, to take it. ¹¹ If

by need you ask it, then ask in humility, for your need is not glory but frailty. [12] If for sport you seek it, you dishonor yourself. And if for glory you take it, you defile yourself. It is not yours, and you are but a robber.

[13] O man, you reign not over the earth, but she is your master through all of your days and your conqueror when the last night falls upon you. [14] You may toil to subdue her, and she may bring forth her bounty, but how great your vanity to imagine that she does so for your pleasure!

[15] There are those who say, "A mere beast has no soul!" Those who say such things understand not the nature of the All. [16] No one has a soul; each one is a soul. So it is also the way with animals. The eyes of every creature serve as gateways to new wonders.

[17] The one who mistreats or neglects a beast is not worthy of your company. If he has no regard for a beast, what regard will he have of you?

[18] The straight path is illusion and the stable foundation will crumble.

[19] Water is supple and creates its own path. Rock is rigid and cracks under pressure. Be like water, which falls down from on high and is carried away by the rivercourse to be gathered by the great water-carrier in seas and lakes and basins. [20] Thence is it cast once again skyward, in secret, and we see it not, to fall once more and renew its blessing.

[21] This is the way of things, no straight path but a cycle in constant renewal. The path unfolds by the way of the wheel, and the journey continues in struggle and repose.

[22] Some say, "Do not strive," and others, "Do not sit idle." Yet the one sits idle not achieves not, and the one who strives always forgoes what is achieved.

[23] Strive for that which is beyond your reach, yet be grateful for all you receive. [24] The one who strives not shall be sacrificed to the passion of others, and the one who is thankless shall be given in sacrifice to his own appetite. Surely shall he be consumed.

[25] Be thankful, yet not content.

[26] Be eager, yet not expectant.

[27] Be vigilant, yet not fearful.

[28] Be strong, yet slow to anger.

[29] Be ready, yet at ease.

[30] Serve all, yet let no man enslave you.

[31] Know yourself, yet seek to learn of others.

[32] The lion hunts but sleeps long. The camel moves slowly, yet endures. The falcon flies, yet cannot run. The sawtooth rides the waves, yet cannot walk. [33] The smallest insect, in sufficient number, can fell the largest tree, and a single idea, which no one can see, may call forth an army that spans the horizon.

[34] It is easier to gaze upon the surface of an onion than to peel away the layers and reveal its inner

meanings. In the same way, it is easier to gaze upon the surface of a man than to seek his true essence - and to stare at the face of an idol than to explore the mysteries behind it.

[35] The one who stays in the center perceives both ends. But take heed, for there is no center between truth and falsehood, between verity and illusion.

4

The Gods

[1] There are those who say that the gods demand to be honored. Yet the gods require not that you honor them, only that you honor your own word.

[2] But some will say, "What if your word is a falsehood?" or "What if it is a word of malice?" Such

questions are folly. What have gods to do with such things?

³ The wise man judges a message not on authority, but on merit.

⁴ There are those who say they hear the voice of a god. It is their own voice they hear, and they are mistaken. ⁵ Yet those who say, "I have never heard such a voice," become a fount of inspiration.

⁶ When a person enslaves his neighbor and says, "My god commanded it," either his god is false or he is.

⁷ When a person mistreats his beloved and says, "My god placed me over her," either his god is false or he is.

⁸ When a soldier plunders his enemy and says, "It is in the name of my god," either his god is false or he is.

⁹ Who are you, O man, to condemn another's god? If that god lives, do you not think he could destroy you with a whisper, mere mortal? And if you say, "It is only an idol," how shall you acquit your own god of like charge?

¹⁰ Do you think that blasphemy offends a god? Do the gods truly care for the babbling of men? And can they not defend their own honor? ¹¹ Indeed, the one who does violence in retribution for such offense brands himself an idiot. ¹² It is bad enough that he shows disdain or his neighbor by doing him violence.

But he heaps scorn upon his own head by presuming his god needs protection. [13] Truly, the contempt he shows his own god and his neighbor shall return to him.

[14] There are those who say, "Do not take the name of a god in vain." Yet these same ones do this very thing when they claim to know the mind of that same god. [15] O, sons of conceit and daughters of treachery! You children of dust speak not of eternity. But from your own minds, you spew forth gibberish and as though you were a prophet. [16] If the god in whose name you speak should hear you, he shall surely upbraid you, and he will close the ears of all to your empty rantings.

[17] Those who pray from rooftops fall from rooftops. As their eyes are ever skyward, their step is never sure.

[18] If all the time spent in prayer for the impossible were devoted instead to achieving the possible, how much richer this world would be!

5

The Priests

¹ The priests of one god spoke of honor. The priests of another preached forgiveness. The priests of a third demanded justice and a fourth, sacrifice.

² Yet their words were false and their motives were impure.

³ Those who spoke of honor had no honor of their own, but offered in its stead false promises and demands of blind loyalty.

⁴ Those who preached forgiveness wished to be forgiven their own cruelty.

⁵ They that demanded justice sought first to define it, and they that called for sacrifice desired that their followers part with their dignity.

⁶ Some said, "Peace!" that their foes might yield; some cried, "War!" that their followers would fight and die in their behalf.

⁷ Here, then, is what you should do when confronted by those of such false virtue:

⁸ Let your honor surpass theirs.

⁹ Forgive yourself first and take not upon yourselves their burden of shame and misplaced guilt.

¹⁰ Serve justice in accord with truth and conscience, not in accord with the lies of those who would reforge it in their own image.

¹¹ Sacrifice in the cause of love and compassion, not in behalf of unyielding dogma.

¹² Seek peace without yielding to tormentors, and seek not war - others will surely bring it to your doorstep in due course.

¹³ They that submit blindly to one who claims authority shall die in darkness, but those who open their eyes to questioning shall live in light.

6

Justice

[1] There are those who say that the sins of the fathers are visited upon the sons. Where, therefore, is justice? [2] If the son is punished for the acts of the father, should the swallow be chastened for the deeds of the hawk? Should the tortoise be judged for the works of the jackal?

[3] Nay, for each one's deeds are his alone, and justice is not mocked by cowards.

[4] The law knows nothing of change. It is written for constancy and cannot awaken to see the new day. [5] The law itself is dead, and like a dead man does not change, save that it decay. It cannot reform its failings; this task is left to those who live.

[6] There are these two things: life and the law.

[7] The law without life is futile. Lacking context, it is like a foreign tongue with no one to translate.

[8] The law without discernment is deadly. It consumes the innocent and guilty alike in its false judgment, and is itself consumed by its passion.

[9] The law is a guardian to life, and so it is that life without law stands in peril. Yet be watchful, lest the guardian turn his sword against the one charged to his keeping.

[10] There are those who say, "Let the scapegoat bear the sins of the guilty one." Where, therefore, is wisdom? [11] The one who blames another for his own folly learns nothing and only repeats it. And each time, an innocent bears his burden. To this there is no end unless the one at fault knows contrition.

[12] Blood does not satisfy vengeance. Desire does not satisfy contrition, and a scapegoat does not satisfy justice.

[13] Forgive not one who asks for solace with a knife behind his back. Turn aside your anger, not your

prudence. Temper fury, but not wisdom. ¹⁴ Only a fool who touches fire seeks again the flame's affliction.

¹⁵ Blame not the innocent for the acts of the guilty. The guilty must bear their burden, and the innocent must be spared. The one who falsely accuses another, and knowingly does so, is as guilty as the one whose acts are in question.

¹⁶ The one who takes credit for the deeds of another is but a vapor. Some say the moon claimed the light of the sun as her own, but was chastened for her hubris with a face consigned to shadow.

¹⁷ The one who blames a demon for his actions is either himself a demon or a scoundrel bent on treachery.

¹⁸ There are those who demand, "An eye for an eye!" Yet they see not their own faults. What, therefore, is the loss of an eye to one already blind? Hypocrites. They ask of others what they themselves can never give.

¹⁹ Those who oft recall a wrong against them inflict upon themselves the way of sorrow.

²⁰ There are those who say, "treat others in such a manner as you yourself would be treated." Yet what is this but vainglory? ²¹ Would the fish of the sea do a kindness by sending the waves to flood the eagle's nest? Would the ploughman favor the herdsman by tethering his ox? ²² Nay, treat others in such a manner

as they themselves would be treated. [23] Think not in your own conceit, "That one is the same I." But learn another's ways and favor him in like manner. In this way do you show kindness and humility.

[24] Some may protest, "There are those who would take advantage of such kindness." [25] Do not put the well being of such ones before your own, but remove yourself from their presence and do not worry about giving them offense. Such ones are already an offense unto themselves.

[26] There are those who make laws and say they are eternal. Yet where were your laws before you walked the earth? And where will they be when you are forgotten?

[27] No minstrel sings lyrics without music. In the same way, no one who sits in judgment should serve law without compassion.

[28] There are those who say, "Black is black and white is white." Yet such ones miss the beauty of the many hues and colors with which the earth is adorned.

[29] There are those who say, "Judge not." Yet without judgement, where is justice? They who judge to share understanding show wisdom. They who judge to exalt themselves are in error.

[30] Do not fear to say, "The thing you have done is an error." But hold your tongue should you be

tempted to say, "The person who has done it is an abomination."

[31] Which does the greater offense, the one who violates an imperfect law or the one acts from malice by seeking to pass through the cracks between the law's letters?

[32] Actions are subject to the judgment of anyone. But the accused are subject only to the judgment of that law which is agreed upon in common and the principles that undergird it. [33] Who can visit punishment upon a deed? It is the doer of the deed who pays the penalty.

[34] Judgment tried and tested strengthens the common good.

[35] Judgment withheld oft turns to deceit.

[36] Judgment imposed by the covetous bears the seed of resentment.

[37] There are those who say, "By the standard you mete out, so shall you likewise be judged." Yet if your standard is just and your heart is true, what place is there for fear?

[38] There are those who say, "I own this land." Yet when your life has ended, the land shall claim dominion over you.

[39] Do you think that the scales of justice are balanced if the same man is acquitted when guilty yet convicted when innocent? May it not be so. Indeed,

both errors weigh just as heavy on the side of transgression.

[40] To tolerate injustice is no virtue. The one who speaks not against an abuser or sits idle in his presence has handed him a weapon more potent than a sword.

[41] Three possible fates await the guilty when sentence is passed: the fate of punishment, the fate of separation and the fate of redemption. The first is the fruit of vengeance, the second is the fruit of fear and the third is the fruit of hope.

[42] The thirst for punishment too often binds the innocent, blinded by the demand for blood and recompense. Separation may preserve the people, and should be used when trust is broken. Redemption holds the richest promise, but have a care, for it also places much faith in the one who may not be worthy. Be sure such a one is deserving.

[43] Blame seeks conclusions. Compassion seeks healing.

7

Instruction

[1] There are those who instruct others how to live, yet they themselves are dead.

[2] To the one who says, "I know," the door is barred. But to the one who says, "I seek," passage is granted. For the first one thinks he need go no further, while the second knows the path leads ever onward.

[3] The teacher who learns nothing from the student is unworthy of the title.

[4] Those who seek the counsel of only the like-minded never know the thoughts of their enemy, and those who revel in flattery never recognize deceit. Such ones are easily vanquished. [5] But those who take heed of adverse opinion see the world from every angle.

[6] Do not say, "This is my teacher." Say instead, "This is my teaching." Do not rely on the authority of others, but let your words carry their own authority.

[7] Do not ask, "Who has sent you?" Instead ask, "What has brought you?"

[8] Ascribe not your own folly to another's lips because you wish to shame him. Let his own folly expose him; otherwise, learn from his wisdom.

[9] The one who makes excuses lacks understanding. The one who seeks understanding has no need for excuses.

8

Family

¹ There are those who say the man is head of the woman. But I ask you: Who was it that gave you birth? Woman was not taken from man, but man from woman. ² Do not boast, therefore, in your strength, O man. But be grateful to she who bore you, for had she cast you aside as an infant, you would surely have perished.

³ The man who sells his daughter in exchange for a dowry treats her like a harlot and dishonors himself. But the daughter so given is not dishonored. Indeed, her honor is ten thousand times that of her father.

⁴ The one who lays an offering on the altar while his family goes hungry defiles the altar and dishonors his name.

⁵ Those who give tithes and offerings while their household is in want are no better than a king who collects taxes from a beggar.

⁶ There are those who say, "Do not divorce your helpmeet." But I say, do not remain bound to one who is poorly suited. It is a kindness to release such a one, and it is folly to remain yoked in deceit and bitterness.

⁷ The foolish judge a person by his birthright, for no one knows how much fruit a tree may bring forth

until the proper season. [8] Would you prize the seed that may never take root and cast aside that which may feed a village? How foolish is such condemnation! [9] Those who rush to judgment deny justice. But more than that, they deny themselves the bounty of a fine harvest.

[10] The one who cuts or brands his children as though they were property has branded himself as a keeper of slaves. Such a one has sacrificed his children to his own vainglory and his honor upon a barren altar.

9

Intimacy

[1] There are those who say, "Do not waste your seed." But one's seed is always replenished. Better instead to worry about wasting your words, which may not be withdrawn or replaced if they are folly.

[2] There are those who say, "Be fruitful and multiply." Yet true fruitfulness lies in acts of honor;

when these are multiplied, they bring a far greater harvest.

³ If a child is brought up among quarrels, he will learn the way of quarreling. If a child is brought up in the presence of anger, she will learn the ways of anger. If a child is raised in a home of true affection, he will not shrink from love.

⁴ If a man lies with a man, what is that to you? If a woman lies with a woman, what offense is given? ⁵ You concern yourself with such things, yet curse your own husband or beat your own wife. You defile another's bed with accusations, yet your own is filled with spite. Behold! It is soaked in blood and fallow. ⁶ When you have fed all the hungry, clothed all the widows, housed all the outcasts and put an end to violence, then you may consider such matters. ⁷ But consider them well before you speak of them, lest the ones you accuse bring their own case against you. If they do, mark this: They surely shall prevail.

⁸ Some speak of man and woman as though they were ice and fire. Yet does not each desire compassion? Indeed, both seek the respect of their neighbors, and both would have others mark their words and treat them kindly. ⁹ Why do you magnify that which is different when so many things are held in common? Each does breath, does think, does laugh, does mourn, does bleed, does sleep, does take sustenance. ¹⁰ Give not so much thought to fine

distinctions. Consider instead this shared life, which binds them.

10

Government

[1] Seek not to place a king over you, for if that one is unworthy, he will pillage your land, and even if he be worthy, his sons may not follow in his ways. [2] Seek instead leaders of wise counsel, whose words are noble and proved by all their actions. May they be women and men of good repute among the people,

and may they be answerable for their edicts to those whom they affect.

³ The one who obeys without question is like the one who says "I see!" without looking, and the one who concedes without trying. ⁴ Such a one has relinquished his soul and become the lapdog of a tyrant.

⁵ The ruler who seeks war for the sake of glory is not fit to rule. The one who seeks war for the sake of gold betrays his people. The peace must be protected, but war should never be pursued.

⁶ Those who rush to war find the path to peace the slowest.

⁷ The one who taxes the people for his own enrichment is a thief.

⁸ The wise leader is truly humble, for true humility casts its eye outward, not inward. It focuses not on the deficiency of self, but on the greatness of the All.

⁹ The one who leads should be the greatest listener, and also the greatest observer. The leader who fails to see and hear what lies ahead leads the people into hardship. The one who heeds not the words and deeds of those behind him will quickly find himself alone.

11

Defilement

[1] There are those who say that the clothes or the hair defile the people. Yet what are clothes and hair but shade and warmth? [2] Those who forbid adornments to no purpose are slaves of vanity, as surely as those who preen and gawk at their own image.

[3] In like manner, there are those who say, "Do not eat this, for it will defile you" and "Do not eat that, for it is forbidden." But each one should eat according to his own conscience and partake according to that one's disposition. [4] It is the one who kills and does not eat who is defiled, for he is a wastrel and a murderer.

[5] If a woman has an issue of blood, she neither defiles nor is she defiled. Do you curse the blood that runs through your veins or the child brought forth from the womb? [6] The blood of life is a blessing and should be celebrated. It is never a cause for shame.

[7] If someone among you should convulse, do not say, "He has a demon" or "This one is cursed." The one who utters such ignorance curses only himself.

[8] You who put wine to your lips when your child goes hungry, how is it that you scoff at a woman

nursing her child. [9] There is nothing sweeter than a mother's milk and nothing more bitter than a man drunk on his own condemnation.

[10] You who find cause to curse your neighbors for their differences, who shall be cursed when their skill and resource exceed your own?

[11] You curse the foreigner. You curse the one who is afflicted. You curse the poor. You curse the one whose belly is large and the one whose frame is lean. [12] You curse the poor and the homeless. You curse the one who rejects your book and the one who affirms another. You curse the one who is too tall or too short, too old or too young. [13] You send them all into exile within your own mind and, if you have the means, to the very ends of the earth. [14] Yet which of these are you? Certainly you are one of them. And just as surely, it is you who are the exile.

[15] The one who laughs at another in spite masks his fear, yet the mask is but illusion and what is hidden shall quickly be manifest. [16] The one who laughs at himself in good humor shows his heart to all the world. There is no mask, no illusion. Such is the way of courage.

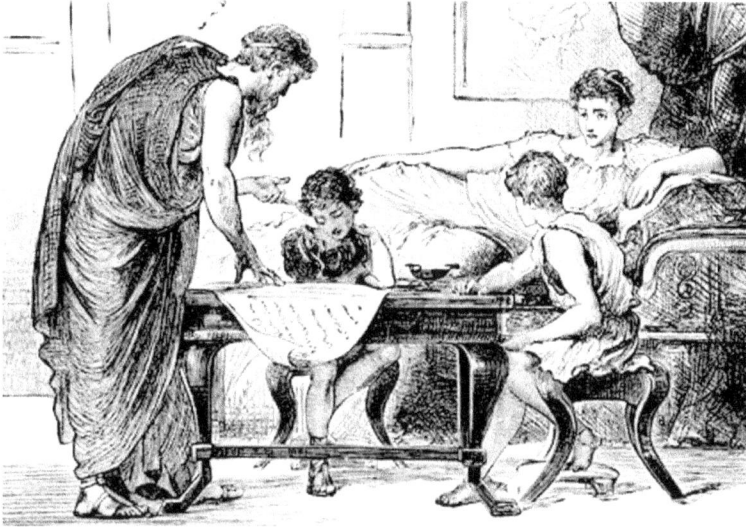

12

Wealth

[1] The one who profits from another's labor is like a tick on the ear of a dog or a wolf in the sheepfold.

[2] The wolf eats only until his belly is full, but the appetite of greed is never sated.

[3] The one who demands payment at high interest is like the landholder who shears his tenant's sheep in winter, then mocks him as he freezes for want of a covering.

[4] The one who buys another's speech with gold buys only falsehood and corruption.

[5] The one whose wealth speaks to silence another has sewn up the mouth of freedom with threads of gold.

[6] The one who lends at interest for profit is a sluggard with nothing of true value. He sells thin air and deals in illusion. [7] Let him earn his keep by the fruit of his labor, the skill of his craft and the sweat of his brow.

[8] It is an irony of ironies that gold is taken from the earth by those who seek to possess the earth, to which they shall at last return.

[9] Bring no sacrifice to any god's altar. The earth shall fall upon you. The skies shall open up and lay siege to you. The sun shall cause you to wither, and the sea shall pull you under. [10] This is your true sacrifice, and all must offer it when their lives are completed.

[11] What use is something offered from the hand which cannot grasp it? Would the one who borrows a fortune from the royal treasury approach the throne with a few coins and call them a gift? [11] Such an act is no gift, but effrontery, and so it is with all your offerings.

[12] Offer nothing save your virtue, and in so offering this, preserve it.

[13] Offer nothing save your honor, and in so offering this, sustain it.

13

Fellowship

[1] Despise not those who are different, for they are your teachers. Cast them not aside, lest they leave you to wallow in your folly.

[2] The one who mocks the foreigner, the maid or the afflicted revels in his own ignorance. Such a one clings to fear as though it were a scabbard, unaware that it is empty.

[3] Some wish to see their own success in the ruin of others, never knowing they are blind.

[4] Some say a child is born wretched and evil, that there is no good within him. Others call the same child pure and good, entirely without blemish. [5] But

what is "good" and what is "evil"? Are they not the deeds of men and women: acts of valor and betrayal, of compassion and of cruelty, of charity and thievery?

[6] An infant has done naught for good or ill ere he departs his mother's womb. How, then, is he blameworthy, and how can he be lauded? [7] A child is neither worthy because he is heir to a kingdom nor wretched because of some ancestor's transgression. Nay, it is a man's deeds that are good or evil, and likewise deeds which do corrupt him.

[8] In battle, the one who inflicts pain upon a captive to gain the advantage is himself captive to an illusion. [9] Thinking he shall be made wiser, he plays the fool. For he knows not that lies are born of desperation, and that deceit pours from the lips of an enemy afflicted.

[10] There are those who say, "Welcome your enemy." Yet they who invite malice are seldom disappointed.

[11] There are those who say, "Welcome the stranger into your home in the cause of hospitality." But does the mole invite the snake or fox into its burrow, though it be a stranger to him? Does the rose invite the aphid to feast on her branches, though the aphid were not known to her? [12] No, welcome not the stranger, but the person of good character. Should an intruder claim your home, and should he claim it,

how then can you offer your hospitality to one truly in need?

[13] There are those who say, "Burn no bridge once you have crossed." Yet what if an enemy pursues you? Better that you burn a bridge behind you than look always over your shoulder. [14] Do not risk stumbling through the darkness with your eyes fixed on the past.

[15] When others bring disgrace upon themselves, be gracious.

[16] When others are fearful because of lies, assuage their fears with truth.

[17] When others revile or extol you, know that these are their perceptions.

[18] There are three sorts of offense. The first is created out of ignorance, the second out of malice and the third from fear. The first is called error, the second cruelty and the third cowardice. [19] Before you accuse or forgive your neighbor, be sure concerning the nature of his transgression - and also his future intent.

[20] If you offend another and are in the wrong, remember this: the effect upon the one you have wronged is the same, regardless of your intent. [21] Therefore let your sorrow be sincere and not bound up with some excuse.

[22] There are those who say a woman should marry the man who takes her by force. Where, then, is

justice? [23] For if a woman is made to accept such a one, his vile deed is magnified. Better for such a one that he be forbidden to marry. Remove such a one far from your daughters.

[24] He who says a woman is less than a man is himself less than a man.

[25] There are those who say the slave is born to his station. But those who speak thusly were never slaves.

[26] The one who makes the most promises is the one least apt to keep them.

[27] The one who gives a gift and seeks its return is like a baker who makes bread for a neighbor, yet demands it back once eaten. [28] He has no cause to complain if he receives it back in a condition far different than its former state.

[29] It takes two sides to make peace, but only one to make war. Yet where the two stand together, they are stronger.

[30] Guard these three things more closely than any treasure: the light in your eyes, the song in your heart and the love of your companion.

14

Appearances

[1] Who are you to say, "Woman, cover your face!" or "Man, shave not your beard!" Is the visage a shame to the either? Or is it not instead your own shame that you seek, in your hubris, to inflict upon them?

[2] If a priest says, "Clothe the poor!" yet dresses in fine raiment of silk and golden cords, of what merit are his words? [3] If a prophet says, "House the orphans!" yet builds a fine temple of marble and cedar for those who follow him, of what value is his entreaty?

[4] A man who seeks perfection is a dog chasing his own tail. All he shall catch is the stench of his own pretense.

[5] The one who judges others according to the manner of their dress is like the one who judges the butterfly according to her cocoon.

[6] The one who upbraids another publicly for a perceived breach of protocol is the one who should be upbraided.

[7] If a man wears his hair long, what is that to you? If a woman dons the garb of a man, what is that to you?

[8] They who seek the favor of nobles for the sake of their own nobility sacrifice it at the feet of those they flatter.

[9] One who hides behind the name of another is no better than a criminal who stows away in the hold of a ship. He seeks free passage at the peril of its owner, endangering also its crew and cargo by his presence.

[10] The first temples were tombs and empty monuments. Your fathers built grand houses for their fathers, while their children found no shelter and starved in squalor.

[11] Pretense is the servant of conceit.

[12] Ostentation is the child of vanity.

[13] Flattery is a bribe and a warning.

15

Speech

[1] Promises are like bridges to the morrow. Never build one without cause, lest you neglect it. And once built, forsake it not, lest it crumble beneath your feet.

[2] The one who boasts lacks surety, but the one who stays quiet shows resolve.

[3] The one who offers an oath betrays want of conviction, either toward his own intent or the trust of another.

⁴ Do you think yourself a prophet? Then you are not one. Do you deem yourself wise? You still have much to learn. Do you claim inspiration? Let it speak on its own behalf. ⁵ The true prophet does not announce himself, but attends to his own soul and speaks through his actions. ⁶ The sage does not shout from the rooftops, but in silence hears the whispers others miss. ⁷ The inspired one believes himself to be ordinary and in the rightness of this belief transforms the world.

⁸ The herald who speaks unbidden in the name of a queen or a king has no excuse. How much greater is the guilt of a self-proclaimed prophet who speaks unbidden in the name of god or goddess?

⁹ If one who speaks hatred in the name of a god, he reveals himself as hateful or his god as the very same. In no wise can hateful speech be godly, any more than the sun can bring forth darkness.

¹⁰ If one speaks destruction in the name of a creator, he speaks nonsense. He might as well spread plague in the name of a healer. ¹¹ The one who destroys a thing simply to rebuild it labors to no purpose, and the one who afflicts a man in order to heal him is a scoundrel.

¹² You look to the stars for answers, yet neglect the heart of the matter within. You search the scrolls for meaning, yet find only that which you wish to see. ¹³ You appoint leaders to guide you, then lay traps for

them to preserve your own conceit. You travel far across the earth in search of glory, yet forget to sing the song that lies within you.

[14] There are those who seek a reward in the next life, but will they find it? Or have they wasted their opportunity in this one?

[15] Yesterday is your teacher; the morrow, your student. Today is the test.

[16] If you want someone to hear you, speak softly. If they do not hear, they were not listening and would not have understood.

[17] The one who bargains with a man who breaks his word is like the one who seeks pleasure from cutting himself on broken glass.

[18] The wise one speaks softly, and others incline their ear to hear them. The slaveholder speaks loudly, and his words are like a swarm of the locusts devouring everything in their path. [19] The one who raises his voice when another disagrees does not seek to be heard, but to be obeyed.

[20] The one who falsely plays the victim makes a victim of those who heed him.

[21] The one who boasts of his own affliction and the one who boasts of his own greatness, how are they different? Each seeks the notice of others, but both are crows calling into the wind.

²² Be thankful for the boaster, who by his bluster makes known his folly. But be on guard against the whisperer, who reveals it not until he strikes.

²³ The snake concealed is more to be feared than the lion that roars. The one who lies in ambush atones for many flaws by way of stealth, and the one who shows all strength betrays his weakness.

²⁴ Fear not the one whose lies are abundant, whose deceit is clear to many. Fear instead the one who leavens truth with subtle falsehood and poisons honor with a single drop of pretense. Such a one is a destroyer.

²⁵ Those who reason together may unlock many gifts wrapped plainly. Yet those who argue stridently in order to prove themselves covet a jeweled box - and scorn its priceless contents.

²⁶ Those who speak in a language beyond your understanding are masters of it. If you deride them for such mastery, you betray only your jealousy. Your true purpose is to mask you own deficiency.

²⁷ Threats are strong poison. If carried out, they kill trust - and perhaps much more. Left unfulfilled they must be swallowed, and are not easily digested.

²⁸ Flattery prepares the way for lies far greater.

²⁹ The gossip speaks not to impart knowledge, but to test it; not to convey information, but to obtain it.

³⁰ Do not give your tongue over to insults. They speak only to your own nature.

[31] Do not give your tongue over to boasting.
It speaks only to your own deficiency.

[32] Do not give your tongue over to cursing.
It speaks only of your own ingratitude.

[33] Do not give your tongue over to gossip.
It speaks only of your own languor.

[34] Do not give your tongue over to rudeness.
It speaks for itself.

16

Faith

¹ There are those who say it is enough to believe. Yet they who believe wrongly rely on their own conceit, and they who believe rightly and fail to act will fare no better.

² Some say, "Those who believe not shall never see." But I say that those who act not shall never know.

³ Some who have faith say, "I have no need of learning, for I know." Some who are learning say, "I have no need of faith, for I am finding out!" ⁴ Yet do these not have faith even so? Their faith is in the mind, their faith is in the senses and their faith is in the journey of discovery.

⁵ Faith untested is like a great feast which no one consumes. It soon grows stale and poisons those who finally partake. ⁶ Those who question do not abandon faith, they test it. And in the testing, they discover whether it is fit to partake.

⁶ Those who believe without seeing and those who see without believing are too often content with seeing half the moon.

⁷ No plan put forth by priest or prophet, by king or captain, by scribe or sage can save you. ⁸ Let your counselors ever be three in number: your conscience,

your wits and your humility. These three things will preserve your honor.

17

Trust and Forgiveness

[1] Loyalty offered a betrayer is like the fattest lamb offered up to the hungriest wolf.

[2] Trust offered a beguiler or a charlatan is like a log thrown on a roaring fire.

[3] There are those who say, "Grant forgiveness to all who seek it." Yet who would open his treasury to all who covet its gold? Surely, such a treasury will soon be empty, and is not your goodwill more valuable than a pile of coins and ingots?

[4] Forgiveness is no simple thing. It is no simple matter of "yes, I forgive" or "no, I do not." [5] As a temple with many courts admits the commoner to the outer square, the priests to the inner courtyard and the high priest to the sanctuary, so it is also with forgiveness. [6] No one admits a supplicant at once to the inner sanctum, lest he consider himself entitled and pollute it. In the same way, offer no betrayer access to your inner keep at once.

[7] Your neighbor may earn your trust in one matter yet be unworthy in another. Make it your practice to know the difference.

[8] The one who withholds forgiveness should take care not to cultivate a crop of bitterness. Grasp its stalk firmly and uproot it, for it is a weed left behind

by the fruit of betrayal. Let nothing of that thing remain to choke the new seeds you have planted.

[9] One who betrays a treaty is unworthy of another. If such a one seeks a new bargain, he must offer a guarantee more valuable than the boon he is seeking. Otherwise, let him wait his turn behind those who have not broken trust.

[10] The one who offers a treaty under threat of invasion deals falsely through coercion. The one who demands obeisance in exchange for salvation knows only tyranny.

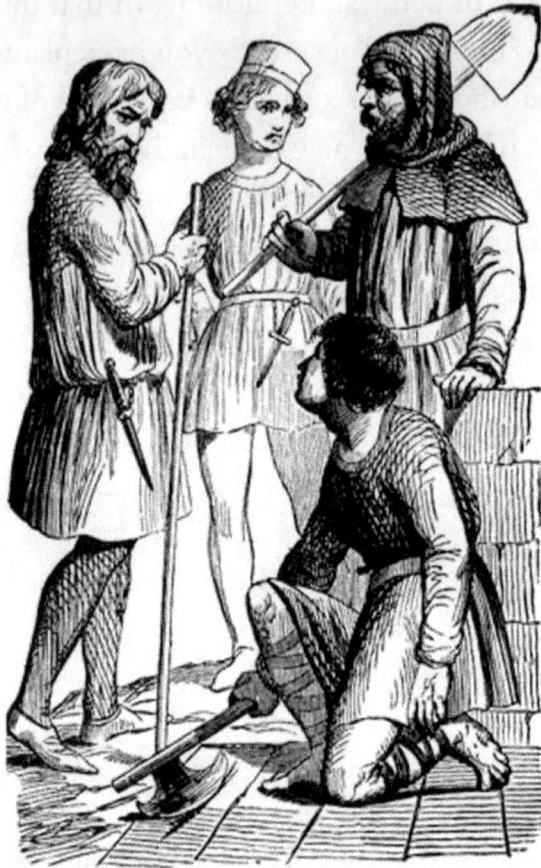

18

Blessings

[1] Blessed are the seekers, for their eyes shall be filled with wonder.

[2] Blessed are the strong of heart, for they shall persevere.

[3] Blessed are the craftsmen, for theirs is an honest living.

[4] Blessed are the artists, for theirs is the work of creation.

[5] Blessed are those of good cheer, for misfortune shall not deter them.

[6] Blessed are the disciples, for they shall not cease from learning.

[7] Blessed are the lovers, for theirs is the secret of the universe.

[8] Blessed are those who know compassion, for theirs is the way of peace.

[9] Blessed is the one who sees with the eyes of a child and reflects with the mind of an elder, for such a one knows wisdom.

19

Exaltations

[1] Exalted are the caregivers, who sacrifice of themselves that others may take comfort.

[2] Exalted are the mediators, who stand on neither side but bridge the chasm between.

[3] Exalted are the healers, who bind the wounds of the afflicted.

[4] Exalted are the scholars, for whom failure is but a stepping-stone.

[5] Exalted are the explorers, who step where others fear to venture.

[6] Exalted are the strangers, who bring new wisdom to those in privation.

[7] Exalted are the protectors, who see that no harm comes to the defenseless.

20

Woes

[1] Woe to you priests and prophets, for you say, "How dare the governor tax the holy treasury!" Yet you yourselves tax the people with tithes to fill your bellies. [2] Hypocrites! You flout the laws of the land in the name of your gods, then replace them with burdens that no one can bear.

[3] Woe to you kings and nobles, hypocrites! For you condemn a man for stealing a morsel of bread, yet set the price so high he cannot meet it. You congratulate the one who steals a fortune, yet condemn the one who takes a pittance. [4] Yet who has done the greater wrong: the one whose lies have made him wealthy or the one whose empty stomach has made him weak? Fools you are, and a fool's reward shall you earn. How safe will your fortune be when the time comes?

[5] Woe to you priests and prophets, hypocrites! You laud those who speak lies in the name of a god but fault them that speak truth for the good of man.

[6] Woe to you priests and nobles, for you give aid to those who prosper and withhold it from the suffering. [7] Fools. The one who does not need your help will forsake you, but the one who is saved by a kindness shall return it.

[8] Woe to you kings and nobles, who tax even the dead to build your fortune. Yet you yourselves are dead already, and you do not even see it.

[9] Woe to you kings and nobles, hypocrites! You steal from the poor to fund your wagers and use the bread of the homeless for a stake at your table. But when your luck runs short, who then will save you?

[10] Woe to you priests and prophets, hypocrites! You preach, "Forgive one another with no expectation!" Yet you yourselves sell forgiveness in exchange for tithes and indulgences. [11] You absolve one debt while incurring another, and so enslave men to you.

[12] Woe to you kings and nobles, hypocrites! For you rob the poor to fund your petty disputes and in the end accomplish nothing. The poor are cheated and your breath is wasted.

[13] Woe to you priests and nobles, for you say, "Thou shalt not kill," yet you slay a man on false charges and make wars on false grounds. [14] You say, "Thou shalt not steal," yet you invade another's land for the sake of plunder. You say, "Honor your father and mother," yet you dishonor them with your deeds.

[15] Woe to you priests and prophets, for you say, "This world is passing away," yet sacrifice your honor to possess it.

[16] Woe to you priests and prophets, hypocrites! You condemn a poor woman for selling her body, yet

sell your very souls for the sake of mammon. [17] Fools. You say the body is a temple, how much more precious is that which resides within? Yet body and soul are one.

[18] Woe to you priests and prophets, for you tremble at tales at ghosts and demons, yet fear not the man or woman whom you have wronged.

[19] Woe to you priests and prophets, hypocrites! For you say the devil appears as an angel of light - a convenient excuse to debase true angels.

[20] Woe to you prophets and seers who say, "It will surely come to pass!" Yet see how quickly the truth betrays you. [21] If you had truly seen tomorrow, would you not have said so plainly? Yet when your words are proven false, you heap more lies atop the first and so compound your error.

21

Instructions

[1] It is written that "You shall have no other god before me." Yet I say, have no other way before compassion and serve no other god but truth.

[2] It is written, "Do not take the name of your god in vain." Yet I say, anyone who dares place his own words in the mouth of a god has already done so.

[3] It is written that you must keep the Sabbath holy. Yet all days are holy, and none should be wasted.

[4] It is written that you should honor your father and mother. Yet I say, honor is greater than kinship.

[5] It is written that you are not to kill. Think hard on this, then, before you send armies beyond your homeland.

[6] It is written that you shall not commit adultery. Yet I say betray no one who is faithful.

[7] It is written that you shall not steal. Yet I say, they who oppress the poor are worse than thieves.

[8] It is written, "You shall not give false testimony against your neighbor." Yet I say, do not stand idle when such testimony is given.

[9] It is written, "You shall not covet." Yet I say, covet kindness, covet smiles and covet virtue.

[10] And I say also to you: Jealousy is but another name for covetousness, so wherefore may a god be jealous?

[11] Some say, "Let your first aim be obedience." Yet I say, let your first aim be understanding. Then after understanding, compassion. Then after compassion, encouragement, aid and sustenance.

[12] Some say, "Give aid for the fear of your god." Yet I say, give aid for the love of your neighbor.

[13] Some say, "Purify your garments." Yet I say, purify your goals.

[14] Some say, "Devote yourself to prayer and fasting." Yet I say, devote yourself to acts of kindness and thanksgiving.

[15] Some say, "Make a journey to the holy place." Yet I say, make the place where you are holy.

[16] Some say, "Shun the heretic and unbeliever." Yet I say, your fear is speaking.

22

Charges

[1] Care then for the children, whose future is your legacy and whose character testifies to your own.

[2] Care also for the elders, who give of themselves that you may prosper.

[3] Care for the earth, who is your mother and provider.

[4] Care also for the creatures who are your companions on this journey.

[5] Let the dew kiss you good morning and the nightingale sing you a lullaby.

[6] Let the road lead you onward, but fear not to explore the hidden paths.

[7] Let the sun warm your shoulders, but cast no shadow on your neighbor's day.

[8] Let your eye be open, your song be joyous, your life be shared and your heart be true.

[9] The one whose eye is ever upon a distant goal risks stumbling over unseen rocks along the path. The one whose eye is ever cast downward for fear of stumbling risks losing his way. Let not one eye be blinded by the other.

[10] Be as a flower, which opens itself to the light.

[11] Be as the ocean, fluid yet unyielding.

[12] Be as the moon, reflective yet illuminating.

[13] Be as the stargazer, always seeking out new light, however distant it may be.

[14] Be as the ship's captain, who knows when to drop anchor and when to ride the waves.

[15] Be as the owl. Cast your gaze in all directions.

[16] Be as the sand crab, at home in shifting sands or pounding surf.

[17] Be as the robin, a herald as winter wanes of better things to come.

[18] Be as the serpent. Shed your skin when it no longer fits you.

[19] Be as the spider. Weave your web and take your leisure.

[20] Be as the leviathan. Plum the depths of your own true waters.

[21] Be as the trees of the forest, sentinels that shade the earth beneath them, that they may be nourished.

[22] Be at rest, that you may awaken.

[23] Be silent, that you may hear.

[24] Be at peace, that you know no distraction.

[25] Be watchful, that your eyes may be opened.

[26] Be supple, that you may bow without cowering.

[27] Be honest, that you may be courageous.

[28] Be joyous, that your joy may be multiplied.

[29] Be steadfast, that you may endure.

[30] Be open, that you may be filled.

23

Paradoxes

[1] The one who seeks to banish chaos withers, yet the one who seeks to escape from order is consumed.

[2] Those who speak of righteous anger believe that they are right, yet more often they are in error.

[3] Existence is confined to a moment, yet that moment cannot be confined.

[4] Solitude is an illusion, yet no one can enter the mind of another.

[5] No man is liable for the sins of his father, yet all too often, he pays for them.

[6] A mystery holds power only so long as it remains a mystery; once understood, it surrenders its power, which is transferred to those who understand it.

[7] These things dance together in tandem. Though two threads, they are a single cord. Though distinct, they are, even so, joined:

[8] The conscious is bound to the hidden self.

[9] Potential and achievement should be two ends of a journey. The first without the second is dross in the wind; the second without the first is a wonder of wonders.

[10] The many are aspects of the one, and the one a product of the many.

[11] Vision without truth is empty, truth without vision is veiled … or absent.

[12] The wondrous is present within the simple, and the simple is itself a wonder.

[13] Light chases darkness, and darkness is the womb that gives birth to that which illumines.

[14] Creation is its own true source, renewing itself throughout all ages.

[15] That which is truly divine transcends the mortal realm through death. It emerges anew, yet only a few may recognize it.

[16] Motion demands substance, and substance is ever in motion.

[17] That which is birthed is also dying, and that which dies gives birth.

[18] The humble are best equipped to go forth with confidence, for true humility is based on truth.

[19] The one who has no convictions can never compromise.

[20] Silence is among the greatest allies of communication.

[21] Harmony is of the greatest use in conflict: those who work best in concert are most likely to prevail.

[22] Tension is the fuel for peace, lethargy an excuse for war.

[23] Hope unfulfilled only magnifies despair; love spurned can turn to hate. Yet the one who is aware renews the source.

[24] Now is the only moment. Yet the one who knows this always transcends it.

[25] One must first acknowledge one's circumstance in order to change it. Mistake not recognition for compliance or anger for determination.

[26] The one who breaks down things for the sake of understanding should know also how to assemble them in the cause of unity. The one who assembles things for the sake of unity should not fear the one who breaks them down for understanding. Analysis and synthesis are partners who work best when in accord.

[27] Science without art is vacant; art without science is a ghost.

[28] That which gives definition must also be flexible, lest it break at the least provocation. That which is flexible yet undefined is but a wisp upon the wind.

[29] Inspiration is to art as vapor is to liquid, different in form yet one in substance. When the liquid is frozen, seek instead the vapor's path.

[30] Those who wake are ever dreaming, and those who dream know not their slumber.

24

Success

¹ These four things bring success: hard work, the help of friends with resource, a shrewd mind and good fortune.

² Without hard work, good fortune is squandered.

³ Without a shrewd mind, work can be to no avail.

⁴ Without luck or favorable friendship, one may toil for years unnoticed.

⁵ Yet all these things together may not be shaken. Nay, all these things together cannot be stopped.

⁶ The one who seeks the All is ever attaining, always releasing.

⁷ Patience waits; persistence acts. Persistence is patience in motion.

⁸ The light-bearer is not concerned with darkness but with finding what it conceals.

⁹ The singer is not concerned with silence, but with the ear that craves her song.

¹⁰ The scribe is not concerned with the empty page, but with the visions to be placed there.

¹¹ The moon without the sun is unseen, but the sun without the moon is constant. Become like the sun.

¹² Which is more potent, the sword or the quill? It depends on the one who wields them.

[13] Which is more fearsome, the shark or the lion? It depends on the place of their meeting.

[14] Which is more noble, the king or the priest? It depends on the condition of their hearts.

[15] Which is more deadly, the brushfire or the cobra? It depends on which one is nearer.

[16] Which is more powerful, a lie or the truth? It depends in some measure on how many believe them.

25

Endings

[1] Some say the world was fashioned in six days, others in years uncounted. Yet it begins always in a single instant, in the moment a new child touches the All.

[2] Some say the world was spoken into being, others that it began with a flash of light, still others in a single breath from the heavens.

[3] Light illuminates being, but light is not the All.

[4] Breath sustains life but does not impart it.

[5] Words bear forth meaning, yet they themselves are not the truth.

[6] The world begins in a moment for each one of us, yet for each one, the moment is different. So the end is also.

[7] Fear not that mountains shall be uprooted or that the seas should rise up in wrath and fury. Fear

not that dragons shall send forth fires from the sky or that the earth shall be opened to consume you.

[8] The end shall not come at a trumpet blast from the heavens, or at the point of fiery swords from some imagined host of hell.

[9] For each, the end is different. Some will meet it in battle, and others on a sickbed. Some will find it in time of joy, and it comes to others in mourning. For some, it is born of vengeance, and for others it is but ill fortune.

[10] For a single one, death is the end of the world. For the world, it is but new beginning.

[11] The womb is a gateway into this world, and death is a passage beyond. You ask what awaits there? Are you vain enough to answer? [12] Does a child know what awaits beyond his first true sanctuary, wherein his mother preserves him? To him, it is all there is. Can he know what, if anything, is waiting for him beyond?

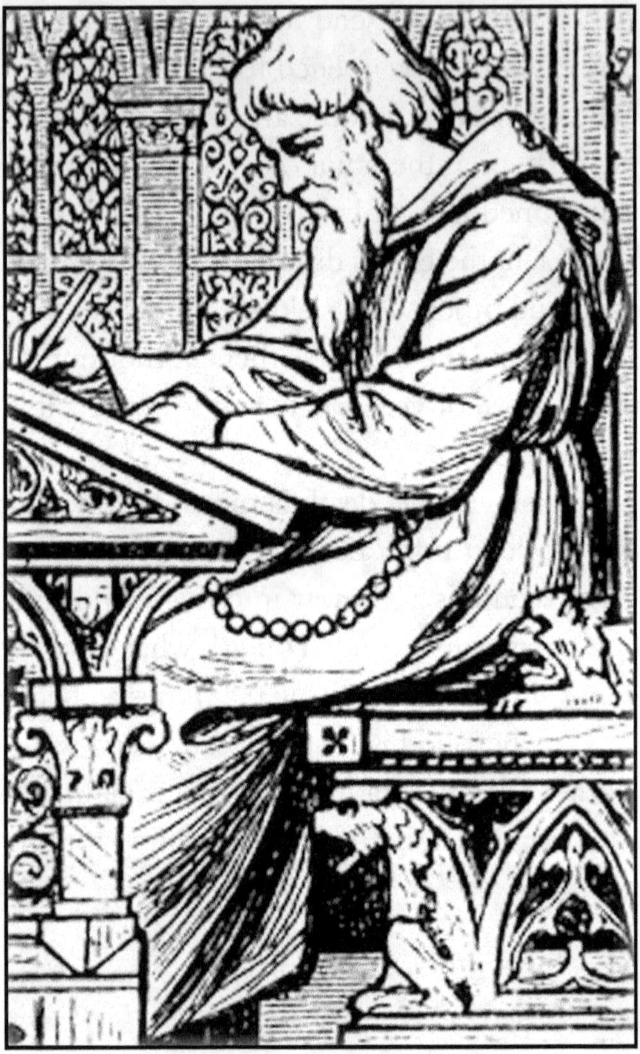

Praise for other works by the author

"The complex idea of mixing morality and mortality is a fresh twist on the human condition. … **Memortality** is one of those books that will incite more questions than it answers. And for fandom, that's a good thing."
— Ricky L. Brown, Amazing Stories

"Punchy and fast paced, **Memortality** reads like a graphic novel. … (Provost's) style makes the trippy landscapes and mind-bending plot points more believable and adds a thrilling edge to this vivid crossover fantasy."
— Foreword Reviews

"Whether a troubled family's curse or the nightmarish hell created by a new kind of A.I., the autopsy of a vampire or Santa's darker side … Provost's sure hand guides you down gloomy avenues you do not expect."
— Mark Onspaugh, author of The Faceless One and Deadlight Jack, on **Nightmare's Eve**

"**Memortality** by Stephen Provost is a highly original, thrilling novel unlike anything else out there."
— David McAfee, bestselling author of 33 A.D., 61 A.D., and 79 A.D.

"Profusely illustrated throughout, **Highway 99** is unreservedly recommended as an essential and core addition to every community and academic library's California History collections."
— California Bookwatch

"As informed and informative as it is entertaining and absorbing, **Fresno Growing Up** is very highly recommended for personal, community, and academic library 20th Century American History collections."
— John Burroughs, Reviewer's Bookwatch

Stephen H. Provost

The author writes about American highways, mutant superheroes, mythic archetypes and pretty much anything he wants. A journalist, historian, philosopher and novelist, he lives on the Central Coast of California. And he loves cats. Read his blogs and keep up with his latest activities at stephenhprovost.com.

www.ingramcontent.com/pod-product-compliance
Lightning Source LLC
LaVergne TN
LVHW021450080426
835509LV00018B/2228